EDUCATION AND THE POLITICS OF DIFFERENCE

EDUCATION AND THE POLITICS OF DIFFERENCE:

Canadian Perspectives

RATNA GHOSH AND ALI A. ABDI

PREFACE BY HENRY GIROUX

Canadian Scholars' Press
Toronto

Education and the Politics of Difference: Canadian Perspectives
Ratna Ghosh and Ali A. Abdi

First published in 2004 by
Canadian Scholars' Press Inc.
180 Bloor Street West, Suite 801
Toronto, Ontario
M5S 2V6

www.cspi.org

Canadian Scholars' Press gratefully acknowledges financial support for our publishing activities from the Government of Canada through the Book Publishing Industry Development Program (BPIDP).

National Library of Canada Cataloguing in Publication

Ghosh, Ratna
    Education and the politics of difference : Canadian
perspectives / Ratna Ghosh and Ali A. Abdi.

Includes bibliographical references.
ISBN 1-55130-266-7

    1. Multicultural education--Canada. 2. Multiculturalism--Canada.
I. Abdi, Ali A. II. Title.

LC1099.5.C3G48 2004   370.117'0971   C2004-901591-5

Cover and text design by Aldo Fierro
Cover photo by jcarter/istockphoto.com

04   05   06   07   08   5   4   3   2   1

Printed and bound in Canada by AGMV Marquis Imprimeur, Inc.

Canadä

TABLE OF CONTENTS

PREFACE

At a time when education is under siege and democracy is in crisis all over the world, Ratna Ghosh and Ali Abdi have written a book of soaring intelligence and conviction. Refusing the growing fundamentalism and racism that often wraps itself in educational reform, *Education and the Politics of Difference* boldly argues that democracy cannot survive without making the politics of difference and multicultural understanding central to any viable notion of critical education.

A substantive and inclusive democracy demands, according to Ghosh and Abdi, more than tolerance. It demands justice as a ethical response to the other, as well as an extension of resources, rights, and recognition to all of those whose very presence and difference expand and deepens the very meaning of freedom, democracy, and equality.

Argued with enormous passion and insight, *Education and the Politics of Difference* insists that bigotry rather than difference is the enemy of democracy. Recognition of this is crucial to educating new generations of students and others engaged in creating a society built on justice and empowerment for all.

This is a brave, comprehensive, and wonderful book full of important insights, analyses, and suggestions for educational reform. Read it with pleasure and pass it on to everybody you know.

—Dr. Henry Giroux
Waterbury Chair Professor of Education and Cultural Studies
Pennsylvania State University

ACKNOWLEDGEMENTS

The practice of acknowledgement in a book can hardly be complete, for any project of this nature involves many more people than the ones mentioned here, who have, in one way or another, contributed to this achievement. In our case especially, as university teachers, we have greatly benefited over the years and in our ongoing intellectual quest, of which this work becomes an important component, from our in-class and other research-based collaborative experiences with our students at both McGill University and the University of Alberta. The 'learning together' project we have undertaken with these developing and, in many cases, rising scholars, have stimulated many critical interactions in teaching and writing about intersections of culture, education, and social development. It is via these interactions with these students that we are continuing to refine our observations and provisional findings.

Ratna Ghosh is particularly indebted to her mother, Mrs. Indira Guha, and her late father, Dr. Gauri Shankar Guha, for the many tangible and intangible ways in which they encouraged her towards the love of scholarship. She would also like to specially thank two of her current doctoral students in the Department of Integrated Studies in Education at McGill University, Ayaz Naseem and Aditya Raj.

It is in that same vein of recognition that Ali A. Abdi would like to thank his doctoral students in the Department of Educational Policy Studies, University of Alberta, who are collaborating with him on topics pertinent to this book, but also extendable to citizenship education, globalization, and postcolonial studies in education. He also wants to thank his wife, Muhubo A Hussein, and his two children, Elyas and Yonis, for their support in this endeavour.

Cheryl Shinfield is thanked for her assistance in editing the manuscript. Thanks are also due to Althea Prince, Managing Editor for Canadian Scholars' Press, not only for her support and patience, but also for the critical and scholarly value she attaches to this book. We also greatly appreciate the insightful comments provided by the two reviewers who have read the work for the publisher.

INTRODUCTION

Education is that which liberates.

—*Sanskrit proverb*

ominant discourses on the role of education in modern democratic societies have centred on its equalizing potential. The attempts at democratizing schools notwithstanding, there seems to be a rethinking of the role of schools and of their moral and political responsibility in contemporary societies. The assertion of ethnicities and cultural identities on a global scale has challenged cultural boundaries and produced tensions in the democratic system. Racism and rightist fundamentalism, poverty and homelessness, the feminization of poverty, family violence, and other human rights abuses are continuously present in society. In some cases, these multi-pronged malaises are tearing at the social fabric of western and non-western democracies alike. This brings into question whether democracy has lost its dynamic vision and has become restricted simply to constitutional principles and institutional organizations. As understood here, democracy is "a system of social relations based on forms of pluralism and popular power that encourage social forms [which] extend and encourage rather than deny the realization of a variety of human capacities" (Giroux, 1991, p. 295). As Giroux (2001) notes again, the practice of democracy in the public sphere is achieved through progressive public schooling that aims for the overall achievement of justice, liberty, and equality that pervade the social and economic as well as the political life of society. This implies a moral imperative and an ethical standing that are significant. The new politics of cultural difference focuses on cultural and political identity as central to the meaning of democracy and democratic representation. To sustain a genuine democratic representation, the new politics of difference focuses on transforming the monolithic and the homogenous into new forms of diversity, multiplicity, and heterogeneity that welcome the contingent, the provincial, and the shifting (West, 1993).

Inequality, or more comprehensively inequity, has been at the centre of political debate in the latter half of the last century, and the issue continues to be discussed as the twenty-first century begins, with special attention accorded to how these constructs are to be defined, operationalized, and lived relative to the dominant group, and with respect to race, gender, social class, and a number of other differences. In education the question has been: can schools—as important institutions for socialization—be the vehicles for achieving the democratic ideals of equality and justice in society? Furthermore, do schools—in policy and practice, as well as in the process of educating—give equal access, equal opportunity, and equal treatment to children of different racial, ethnic, gender, and social class backgrounds? Do schools create the conditions necessary for critical literacy for *all* children—and not simply for the children of privileged groups? Are teacher education programs responding to the needs of the changing societal and school demographics in the preparation of teachers in a diverse society?

The need for a moral and political dimension in democratic discourses implies that the vision extends beyond equality issues, and should enable citizens to participate in the creation and recreation of a critical democracy. Equality is a necessary, but not sufficient, condition of social and educational life. To safeguard the principles of justice and equality requires the empowerment of the individual and, where relevant, the collective. In the literal sense, to empower is to enable, to develop the ability to do. In education it refers to "the ability to think and act critically" (Giroux, 1992, p. 11). Are educators aware of the ethical responsibilities and political implications that education for a critical democracy implies? To answer this and similar questions, we should realize that even the fundamentals of equality, especially in the conventional sense, which focused on the equalization of the fiscal and physical (facilities, supplies, etc.) aspects of the issues, are no longer enough to disturb the problematic contours of contemporary learning arrangements.

Equality must now be concomitant with, or preceded, even superseded, by the conceptual as well as the practical realities of equity (Abdi, 2001a). As such, and based on our purposes in this work, equality could actually be subsumed into the conceptual and practical constructions of equity, which, as the more inclusive term, could represent all the policy and programmatic cases of education and other re-distributive societal possibilities that should aim for a comprehensive social justice. To implicate the increasingly converging analysis of the two terms, though, we have been liberal with their usage, thus deploying them interchangeably, or even as demanded by specific observations and discussions. It is also important to understand that in many instances, both equity and equality could represent, depending on the nature of societal and other needs, the desired and multidimensional levelling of resources and other desired possibilities in any given situation. As more focused perspectives on the critical as well as the functional structures of the two concepts and their practices are discussed in education, their distinctive usage and/or selectively descriptive amalgamation would become, we expect, more common and objectively less nuanced.

To discuss these and related topics, we must understand that the social sciences, in the past several decades, have been through a tremendous epistemological turmoil resulting in widespread methodological reorganization. The break from positivist/structuralist philosophy (or modes of thought) and epistemology (the theory of knowledge) towards a critical social science represents a revolutionary shift. This shift is one from the conventional positivist/structuralist paradigm towards a critical paradigm. This is a dramatic shift because it questions the very assumptions of the production and the meaning of knowledge, argues for analysis of history, and relates knowledge to power. This paradigm shift represents a challenge to an ideology that previously gave legitimacy to only one section of society rather than represent the variety of human experiences. As Giroux (1981) pointed out, that ideology, which is a value-laden view of the world, becomes hegemonic when it is institutionalized by the dominant group to legitimize existing practices.

While progress has been made in the numerous attempts to challenge the dominant paradigm, the case is not complete yet and most contemporary educational discourses and practices continue to be dominated by the structuralist and positivist epistemologies (McLaren, 1997). Despite this reality, though, many educators, especially those in Western democracies, are becoming increasingly involved in the theoretical debates in the social sciences and their implications for the process of education, both for students and teachers. But there is still a great need in education to integrate conventions of knowing, believing, and working; that is, in the epistemology, ideology, and methodology of teaching and learning.

The call for schools that do not reproduce the status quo is in response to a relative perception of a crisis in those schools. This is supported by studies that indicate high illiteracy and dropout rates, student boredom and resistance, and increasing crime and drug dependence among youth, not to mention general confusion in values and moral standards. The already emergent, progressive trend in education testifies to the perceived inadequacy of the existing educational system to deal with the tensions that are rooted in society. In particular, poststructuralist, humanist educators are concerned with an educational philosophy and process that excludes different groups of students (females, minority cultures, members of the working class, and others) and that thus contributes to social inequality and injustice. Traditionally, the worldview and experiences of the dominant group have been perceived to be universal knowledge and as representing the situation of all children. The varied consciousness, history, and experiences resulting from differences—in terms of gender, ethnicity, and class—which have been previously ignored as knowledge, and demeaned as inferior or inappropriate in comparison to the conventional knowledge transmitted in the schools, are slowly but steadily gaining legitimacy. Conventional, Western-based knowledge portrays a particular Eurocentric worldview. The theoretical challenge to traditional knowledge and meaning, and the progressive trend in education to include the history, the lived experiences, and the consciousness of those who are different from the traditionally dominant group, could therefore be selectively viewed as a paradigm shift.

In his influential book *The Structure of Scientific Revolution* (1976), Thomas Kuhn showed that every scientific breakthrough is a break with traditional ways of thinking, with traditional paradigms. He defined a paradigm as a framework for perceiving and understanding a field, a cognitive structure or a lens through which problems are looked at and that reflects our view of the world. It is when inconsistencies are evident, or when a crisis occurs, that people begin to question the adequacy of the prevailing paradigm and that a new paradigm appears. The prevailing paradigm in education claims to provide equality of opportunity but does not allow for the attainment of the goals of equality either in practice or through the curriculum. As in other professional fields such as medicine and law, the focus in education is on practice, and educational paradigms must, therefore, include practical action along with theoretical knowledge. As such, the key question will always remain whether a prevailing paradigm serves the purpose of education. This will depend on how the goals and purposes of education are defined.

In western societies and especially in North America, the traditional goal in education has been the transmission of the dominant culture, involving assimilation for those who were different. The critical perspectives and new theoretical insights point to a break with the assimilation paradigm, replacing it with a radically new way of thinking in terms of a multicultural frame of reference. The inconsistencies evident in an assimilationist approach in democratic, heterogeneous, and immigrant societies have initiated questions regarding the adequacy of the prevailing paradigm. The crisis in education makes a new paradigm imperative. Multiculturalism represents a paradigm shift because it involves a new ideology and a radically new way of thinking in education. More importantly, polycentric multiculturalism, or multiculturalism with many centres (Stam and Shohat, 1995), hastens, and in the process contextualizes, the new paradigm shift. Hence, the paradigm conflict that arises between assimilation and multicultural education. The two constitute different values, discourses, practices, and visions of society and reality emanating from particular philosophies and political ideologies. The goals and functions are different, and to understand the polarity involved, we must recognize their differences. To minimize those differences is to ensure the continuation of the status quo.

This book selectively discusses the significance and implications of this paradigm shift in teaching and learning. It attempts to narrow the gap between the dramatic theoretical developments in the social sciences and the concept of multiculturalism, and difference-friendly multicultural education. In sketching the ground for such a project, this book will explore how conceptions of difference and knowledge converge and suggest a restructured vision of multicultural education as an important site for cultural transformation.

The focus here is theory, although both theory and practice concern pedagogy. Theory explains relationships: between knowledge and power, education and society. Furthermore, it explains cultural differences in students (based on race/class/gender), their educational performance, and their future. Practice shows how the process of schooling signifies and represents the relationship between educational performance and cultural differences. As such, genuine multicultural education would involve the psychological as well as the cultural relocation of teachers in the class so that student-teacher interactions become relatively equalized, dialogic and responsive to the specific needs of the learner (Ghosh, 1996). Theory and practice reveal the politics of culture and difference, because schooling "involve[s] the very nature of the connections between cultural visions and differential power" generally undertaken via the continuing legitimization of select texts and bodies of knowledge (Apple, 1992, p. 7).

The first chapter of the book traces the dramatic changes in the concept of education's role in society in terms of its equalizing and equiticizing potential, and the revolutionary shift in the concept of knowledge. It then problematizes the concepts of difference and identity as points of departure for reconceptualizing multicultural education to allow full development of the potential and critical abilities of all children regardless of their differences. In the context of this book, the terms "difference" and "Other" will refer to the conceptualization of groups based on racial, ethnic, gender, and social class characteristics, although we are cognisant that there are other socially or otherwise based differences. It is also important to note that in the analysis and stated or intended definitions in this work, identity is assumed to mean the individual or the groups', conceptualizations and related livelihood practices that define who people are. In addition, we agree with Taylor (1994) that in order for identity to be authentic, the subject of that identity must be the source of his or her identity. When that is not the case, the notion and its praxis become non-authentic, basically imputed, and arbitrarily imposed identity (Abdi, 2001b). Taylor (1994) notes that in such cases, the resulting misrecognition could bring about a possible cluster of negative consequences for overall individual and social development. As such, the type of difference-accepting multicultural education that is discussed in this work has to foster authentic identity, which would eventually enhance transformative possibilities for all learners, especially those who are marginalized in conventional, monocultural settings of teaching and learning. Clearly then, we are not presenting multicultural education and identity as simply quasi-related discursive entities, but with the pragmatic understanding that the latter could be a select sub-set of, and contextually operationalized within, the analytical structures and educational possibilities of the former.

Again, identity may still come across as an ambiguous concept. Educators need to understand the complexities and dynamics underlying the construction of identities because of their significance in the development of ideologies of nationalism, ethnicity, and student self-concept. Individual experiences intersect with class, colour, and culture, and are embedded in history. Social distance or ranking is constructed not only on gender and race/ethnicity axes, but also on the socio-economic and educational ones. Indeed, as a dynamic and key element of subjective reality, identity has a dialectical relationship with individuals as well as with society.

The second chapter focuses on select perspectives of multicultural education, and again discursively analyzes notions of equity and equality in education. Here, the perspectival approach is still theoretical, with such multicultural education-related issues as race (not as a biological entity but as a socially constructed category), gender and social class discussed. Assuming, for the purposes of our analyses, that prejudices that are either race, gender, or class-based could lead to discrimination, the chapter attempts to relate these issues to the possible role of multicultural education in positively dealing with difference, in constructing viable pluralistic identities, and in, eventually, empowering students who would otherwise feel disempowered and may disengage from the practice of schooling. Primarily due to the temporally and spatially fluid nature of the points addressed in this chapter, its organizational structure may be, at times, quasi-eclectic, with some of the themes already presented reappearing in subsequent discussions. That is to be expected in the analysis of educational problems and possibilities in any society that is culturally evolving, with policies and programs cyclically influencing each other.

The third chapter represents a historical and contemporary discussion of multiculturalism and multicultural education in Canada. The chapter starts with an overview of past problems of Canadian immigration, and traces the evolutionary nature of the changes that have taken place over the years. Indeed, as is demonstrated here, a country that had a clearly racist immigration policy up until recently, has now embraced one of the most progressive programs of immigration and refugee systems. While that should be welcomed, it is also clear that the rapidly changing structure of the Canadian ethnic and racial makeup poses a number of culture and education-related concerns that must be addressed. Moreover, the chapter takes a special look at the unique case of Quebec's intercultural policy that promotes—in fact, establishes—the supremacy of the French language and culture in all matters educational in the province. Explicitly stated in the Quebec case is that all immigrants and refugees who choose to live in that province, regardless of their background, will be a part of Quebec society, with integration and related issues achieved through the primary categories of the province's culture. In addition, this chapter discusses the historically tragic but slowly improving case of Aboriginal education, with special focus on the myriad of overall livelihood, cultural, and learning problems that the First Nations people have experienced and are still experiencing. Here, it is becoming clearer that the best possible way out of these enduring regimes of deprivation could come through Aboriginal communities assuming control of their education, and using it to revive their cultures, languages, and select components of their social and psychological development.

The fourth chapter discusses education and the globalization of difference. If the movements of people, goods, and services has now taken an increasingly expanding global dimension, then education's role to deal with these massive international and inter-continental intermixes and the resulting intermeshing of cultures, languages, religions, and related lifestyles also calls for the introduction of new learning philosophies and practices. These new educational roles, which will be based, at least in Western democracies such as Canada, on the conceptual and pragmatic notions of multiculturalism, would go beyond just accommodating or tolerating the different baggage that new groups and individuals are bringing with them. Educating for difference in the global context will assume new ways of valuating other people's cultures, histories, and the unique ways they manage their lives, and accepting—always within the prescribed boundaries of the law—beliefs and behaviours that, if appreciated, would undoubtedly enrich the multicultural fabric of these societies. One segment of the chapter focuses on the so-called new world created by the September 11, 2001 terrorist attack in the United States. One point raised in the discussion of these events is that while the world has to safeguard against these types of tragedies, one important way to prevent them in the long run is to establish inclusive and culturally multi-centric educational possibilities that effectively highlight the positive aspects of global coexistence, respect for people's different ways of managing their lives, and the creation of new forums of knowledge-sharing among people of different faiths. The aim of this would be to pre-empt, as much as possible, destructive doctrines masquerading as legitimate grievances and all the dangerous and desta-bilizing calculations these could unleash in many parts of the world.

The fifth and last chapter of the book deals with the promise of multicultural education as an important learning tool that can transform the sometimes problematic ways that people from differ-ent backgrounds relate to one another, learn together and, of course, live together. In increasingly multicultural Western democracies such as Canada and the United States, there is no alternative to the ideals as well as the possible practices of multiculturalism and multicultural education. This does not at all mean that dominant groups in these societies whose ideas and programs would greatly influence public policy always welcome these issues. In fact, as Mackey (1998) notes, in the Canadian case (which is arguably one of the most admirable multicultural possibilities in the world), the reality of the heterogeneous social makeup does not discourage many from the dominant segments of society to yearn for the conti-nuities of a quasi-homogenous social order that, at best, selectively tolerates any disturbing cultural variances. That being as it is, one could also state that Canada has come a long way in achieving its multicultural price, and despite all the nostalgia for the old order, the promise of effectively and constructively managing difference and promoting the positive world of polycentric multiculturalism would minimally keep the country's still highly unequal but selec-tively equiticizing cultural mosaic adrift in the direction of true multiculturalism and less symbolic but effectively program-driven components of multicultural education. In all, this book combines select and critically intervening notions of postmodern, postcolonial, and cultural studies to situate aspects of education that should multiculturally, but also effectively, mediate difference and diversity both in the Canadian and global social and learning situations. As such, the book might persuade us to rethink these and related issues through lenses that connect the local to the global, and, of course, the global to the local.

1 | SCHOOLING AND SOCIETY: PERSPECTIVES ON KNOWLEDGE, CULTURE, AND DIFFERENCE

Education, if formulated and implemented with the practices of justice and equity, is the great engine of social development.

—*Nelson Mandela*

Inquiries in the social sciences have produced substantial research on the relationship between school and society, specifically between the knowledge transmitted by schools, and societal position and power. Some traditions of schooling and theories on the social construction of knowledge imply that constructions of reality, their selection, and their organization legitimize the knowledge and culture of the dominant group, with the resulting elevation and ensured continuity of this group's bodies of knowledge at the expense of others (Apple, 2000; Banks, 1993).

The process by which this happens through the agency of the public schools is a complex one. As societies have experienced social, economic, and political shifts as well as globalization-induced movements, there has been a critical public debate over the role of educators and educational institutions. Schools have also been the domain of intense conflict in the controversy over whose knowledge and culture are to be communicated. In heterogeneous societies, education plays a significant role in the development of moral and political skills necessary to pursue a democratic vision of the common good. The issues are political because they involve power struggles among different groups, and conflict with democratic ideals of equal and just participation by all groups. In schools, as in society, power is exercised through the hierarchical classification of differences as binary opposites (i.e., man/woman; rich/poor; black/white) to which meaning is given through social construction. These meanings and stereotypes are rigid and hierarchical, but remain concealed in the ideology of the school and society.

The expansion of mass education, complemented by global migrations and the mixing of people from previously detached geographies, has resulted in heterogeneity of the student population. In North America, the dramatic change in the elite and male nature of schools with universal education is exacerbated because its history is closely linked to immigration. Difference is not only based on the inclusion of female and working class students, but also on racial, ethnic, and cultural diversity. At stake is the equality issue in modern democracies—due to the inclusion of the other—and the school's role as an equalizing force. An education founded on the democratic principles of equality and social justice, however, involves an emancipatory vision of all segments and members of the community (Giroux, 2002). This goes well beyond pedagogical skills for economic and citizenship requirements, and includes ethical and moral issues that will work towards human freedom. An equitable and just community is not necessarily an ethical and caring community. Legislation and regulations do not guarantee the transformation of the societal vision. The need is for change in the affective, ethical, and cognitive domains. As such, in an age of global interdependence, the concept of one world economy, one earth, one environment, one humanity can be cultivated through the ethical dimensions of caring and compassion, and not merely because of pragmatic reasons (Nussbaum, 1998). To achieve this in tangible measure, one must take into account the new expansive possibilities that must be undertaken with a higher sense of sustainable economic development, equitable distribution of resources, overall social justice, and attendant security guarantees for all segments of society. The point is to change the world positively while still seeking new possibilities. Education must help us understand the world in order to change it. To achieve this, we must ask a number of critical questions, including, for example, why are various others systematically marginalized? What changes would bring about a more just society in which all humans would have the right to define the terms of their existence? How can education advance the welfare and interests of all who inhabit this earth?

THE ROLE OF EDUCATION

At least three groups of educational theorists have influenced the main forums that analyzed the role as well as the objectives of education in society, before the first initiatives to challenge the old order began in earnest. The first of these were the consensus theorists, who viewed education's role as that of cultural transmission and human capital formation. These traditional theories remained relatively unchanged in a number of educational settings until the 1960s. They emphasized consensus and viewed the school as providing equal access. Several other researchers began to emphasize the legitimization of the inequality function of the school system through supposedly objective testing, which made unequal results of different groups appear justifiable. The transmission of culture model was seen by conflict theorists as depoliticizing differences as well as the function and process of schooling, because of the connection between knowledge and power. The debate over inequality had shifted from the liberal to the socialist interpretation of equality.

The second group were the structuralist-functionalists (people like Talcott Parsons and Robert Merton) who analyzed inequalities of educational opportunities in terms of assimilation in education and society, and human resource development as a means of gaining mobility by maintaining equilibrium in society. Differences were neither accepted nor considered important. They were deficiencies that could be overcome, and to which non-dominant individuals and groups could aspire if they were successfully shaped in the mold of the dominant group.

The third group of theorists were those who espoused liberal views and who based their assumptions on an ideology of cultural pluralism. They saw adaptation by the dominant group as the means to enable disadvantaged groups to gain access to status as well as economic and political power. Cultural pluralists accepted the plurality of society in terms of fragmented groups—based on racial and ethnocultural characteristics—and recognized the correspondence between the groups, and socio-economic status and class. Here, the dominant group would make some overtures to help subordinate groups adjust. However, the ideal to be achieved was to attain the dominant group characteristics, by which others would be measured for entrance to dominant social institutions. As such, these educational theories were, unlike current multicultural education programs that welcome and accept differences, structurally oblivious to them and, by commission and omission, disguised the exclusion of the other.

To challenge the normalized but problematic corridors of writing and provision, radical theorists, for example, explained the persistence of inequality by viewing the school's role essentially as reproducing the dominant ideology through maintenance of the hierarchical structures in society. Borrowing from the earlier theories of the German social theorists Karl Marx and Max Weber, these thinkers not only saw the problematic of the habitualized continuities of educational and related inequalities in society, but also realized the urgency with which new and inclusive discursive as well as practical platforms should be created if the dominant ideology was ever to be diluted. In addition, correspondence theorists such as Bowles and Gintis, in their well-known work *Schooling in Capitalist America* (1976), pointed out how the hierarchical structure of values is reflected in classroom interactions. There were also a number of independent researchers such as John Ogbu (1992), who made the distinction between class and minority group problems in education and society. Ogbu used the term *caste-like minorities* to describe the structural legacy of some minority groups, and distinguished their educational and economic problems from those of the working class.

With the introduction of issues other than social class-based economics directly influencing education, perspectives on cultural reproduction and the important role of cultural capital as the ensemble of all linguistic and expressive skills children learn from their family and social environments gained momentum primarily with the work of the prominent French sociologist Pierre Bourdieu (1973, with Passeron, 1990). These important works were complemented by Bernstein's (1971) work on language codes in education that had detrimental effects on the learning success of minority students, and by Willis' landmark book, *Learning to Labour*, which showed how conventional programs of learning were, in effect, making sure that the dominant order was maintained by preparing, for example, working class children to find working class jobs, thus discounting any possibilities for viable social mobility and concomitant social advancement. The sustainability of the theoretical threads created by these earlier works was strengthened, through the 1970s and into the current debate on the problems of education as an agent of social development, by the related works of critical theorists (mainly from the Frankfurt School) such as Max Horkheimer (1972), Herbert Marcuse (1964), and Jürgen Habermas (1979).

Over the last decades, a number of studies have utilized critical theory from the humanities and social sciences to focus on culture and cultural production through the daily experiences of teachers and students. Integrating neo-Marxist social theory with microcosmic descriptions of everyday life, they illustrate the dynamics of accommodation, conflict, and resistance that shape the often antagonistic daily experiences of students and teachers' lives (McRobbie, 1991). Cultural resistance involves opposition to dominant cultural codes, or withdrawal from one's assigned position in society. It poses a challenge to dominant patterns of gender, class, ethnicity, and forms of oppression; for example, white, middle class control or male domination. Resistance theories focus their attention on oppressed groups and emphasize human agency or action in the internal workings of the school (McLaren, 1994). One of the weaknesses in resistance theories has been the lack of historical analyses of the conditions that give rise to simultaneous modes of resistance and struggle. Again, challenging a developmentally restraining school environment with any attendant immediacy may be the best option, especially when conditions of life do not allow for the long-term study and analysis of why things are what they are. Here, the main point, *ipso facto*, becomes what one can do now to alleviate current regimes of deprivation that are directly affecting people's lives. The emergence of postmodern theories, primarily through the widely diffused writings of French thinkers such as Jacques Derrida (1976) and Jean-François Lyotard (1984) would also have a lasting impact on how education and knowledge are defined, even if they were not intended to do so in the first place. Postmodern theory, as anti-modernity (modernity as an enlightenment-driven project) usually accords legitimacy, at least theoretically, on all forms of knowledge and ways of knowing. In addition, the analytical as well as the temporal relationships between these and the previous theories, as well as philosophical and discursive attachments, all would have to do with the now *au courant* postcolonial studies area (e.g. Achebe, 2000; Said, 1993, 2000; Bhabha, 1994; Ashcroft et al., 1995). In the new cultural and educational formations that have emerged, not only from education but also from other social science disciplines (poststructuralism, postmodernism, postcolonialism, etc.), the most important pedagogical and knowledge/power deconstructions and reconstructions would involve (a) the delegitimization of meta-narratives or overarching philosophies that are meant to represent universal truths; (b) the emphasis on a cultural politics of difference; and (c) a new and apparently sustainable focus on identity, culture, and power.

Protesting the lack of vision and strategies, as well as gender bias in radical theories, critical radical educators have taken the opportunity provided by contemporary social theories to start to question the knowledge produced in schools and its impact on students of different backgrounds. These theories have enabled educators to rethink the purpose of schooling, and the means by which one can struggle for social justice. Over the past fifteen years, critical pedagogy and a critical feminist pedagogy have been emerging, based on a wide variety of writings. These are inspired by the analytical forces of the Frankfurt School as well as the work of the postmodern scholars and students, with the added but conjecturally primary support of educational philosophers and thinkers such as John Dewey (1952, 1929), Paulo Freire (1985, 1998, 2000), and Antonio Gramsci (1990). Dewey was indeed ahead of his time in advocating for a culturally inclusive education, albeit one with more Euro-American platforms, which was to allow the child to slowly integrate into the new school environment while still expecting to see something of his or her background in the different structures of schooling.

The works of these theorists were again complemented by the important and gender-sensitive books of a number of writers who first highlighted the world of women in educational settings (see, among others, Gilligan, 1982; Lorde, 1984; DeLauretis, 1987; Lewis,

1990; Luke and Gore, 1992; hooks, 1984; Narayan and Harding, 2000). Here again, in the same way that liberal theories of education were challenged from the margins, liberal feminist perspectives that initially formed the vanguard of the movement met new schemes of resistance from, among others, coloured women, who correctly pointed out that analysis of difference solely on the basis of gender was not enough to deal with the multiple levels of marginalization that many women faced. In addition, the new crop of feminist scholars highlighted the fact that mainstream Western women cannot represent the voice of women from Third World countries or those who could be, for a variety of reasons, marginalized in industrialized Western democracies (Collins, 2000 [1990]; Mohanty, 1995). Critiquing the case from the assumed perspective of Third World women, Mohanty writes:

> [In the Western, liberal feminist discourse], a homogenous notion of the oppression of women as a group is assumed, which, in turn, produces the image of an 'average third world woman.' This average third world woman leads an essentially truncated life based on her feminine gender (read: sexually constrained), and being 'third world' (read: ignorant, poor, uneducated, tradition-bound, domestic, family-oriented, victimized, etc.). This, I suggest, is in contrast to the (implicit) self-representation of Western women as educated, modern, as having control over their own bodies and sexualities, and the freedom to make their own decisions .... These distinctions are made on the basis of the privileging of a particular group as the norm or referent [with Western feminists constructing] themselves as the referent in such a binary analytic (1995, p. 261).

With these clusters of empowering approaches to education for traditionally disadvantaged groups, the very identity of power brokers is at stake, thus implying a change in relations between the traditionally powerful and powerless. Critical pedagogy not only challenges racism, sexism, and classism, but changes the precepts of their foundation. It also implies an integrated society and classroom in which differences do not divide individuals or groups. Hence, the continuing focus on the development of critical citizenry as well as literacy programs that tangibly focus on the relationship between education, learning possibilities, and public enfranchisement (Giroux, 2001).

The now-established literature on critical pedagogy reveals a variety of discourses. Two main strands can be identified. Both are associated with a socialist vision and based on a critique of dominant approaches to education (Gore, 1993). One stresses social vision and sees the role of the school as being a site for equality and social justice. Pointing out that a critique of schools is not enough, it stresses the need to speak the language of possibility and hope in order to change the system and debunk the myth of equality in the present system.

The second strand, represented by those who focus on pedagogy as classroom practice, is consistent with the politics of liberation, and epitomized as a struggle against injustice and inequality. This is undoubtedly influenced by the writings of the late Brazilian philosopher, Paulo Freire (1985, 2000 [1970]). Although Freire's radical pedagogy has been criticized as having neglected gender issues (Weiler, 1991), his broad social vision, symbolized by Third World politics and identity, corresponds with the politics and social vision of critical as well as feminist pedagogy, and can be adapted, across many cultures, into pedagogical practices.

Theories of critical pedagogy are united in focusing on a program that aims to empower those who have been and are being subjected to the equalities and inequities that, more often than not, permeate public spaces and programs of education (McLaren, 1994; 1997). While these theories reveal a diversity in emphasis, they are bound together by their common concern with race, class, and gender oppression. Multiculturalism thus becomes an integral part of the critical pedagogy program. It offers possibilities to educators for going beyond the apolitical and ahistorical conceptions of multicultural education, and instead enables them to focus on issues of power, subordination, and struggle within a progressive vision, which includes both theory and practice. In these critical theories of production, knowledge is considered to be a major productive force of schools. The legitimization, organization, and distribution of the functions of knowledge by schools results in a social hierarchy based on difference. This makes knowledge an object for investigation.

THE CONCEPT OF KNOWLEDGE

Theories of Knowledge

Knowledge characterizes the way we look at the world. Where we are located in society affects how we understand the world. In traditional educational theories, an assimilationist model of education, rooted in the positivist period, insisted on one truth because it was assumed that there was one way of knowing, and knowledge was thought to be value-free. The connection between knowledge and power was not made. In critical pedagogy, of which multiculturalism must be an integral component, knowledge and power are inherently connected. Truth is based on different ways of knowing, made more complex as a result of differences in human experience. The function of knowledge is to lead one towards freedom, and that can only happen when it increases awareness of the hidden aspects of power. That is, when it deliberately diffuses and accords emancipatory knowledge.

Philosophical and epistemological debates have raged through both the social and natural sciences. While realists have argued for universal knowledge that is value-free and neutral, idealists argued that knowledge (in the physical as well as in the social sciences) is contextual, defined by socio-cultural and historical forces. Therefore, it is neither neutral nor value-free. For Freire, knowledge is praxis, primarily for use in action. Knowledge is to be used by marginalized people to change their situation of oppression by challenging the knowledge of the oppressor. This, indeed, is where Freire's well-known program of conscientization (see Freire, 2000 [1970]) comes along. Here, as people become conscious of the conditions as well as the nature of their oppression, they acquire the critical faculties to proactively respond to their relationship with their social and physical environments, becoming capable, in the process, of transforming their lives vis-à-vis their oppressors. In the newly forming, post-conscientization contexts, knowledge is interpreted by its purpose, and produced in a manner that is multi-perspectively relational. As Lusted (1986, p. 4) pointed out earlier, "Knowledge is not the matter that is offered so much as the matter that is understood."

In addition, feminist pedagogy is also largely a response to the traditional theory of knowledge in which the white middle class male (classified as the norm) represents all human experience as universal (validating certain methodologies). Pointing out that what is claimed as universal is largely inapplicable to the historical experiences of women (and peoples of other races, ethnicities, and classes), feminist scholars raised questions about the kind of knowledge and the particular means available to men for obtaining universal knowledge. In an attempt to put women's experiences within a broad framework of human civilization, feminist scholarship points to the social, historical, and political aspects in the construction of knowledge.

Knowledge in Educational Theories

Critical pedagogy demands a reformulation of theories of knowledge that focus on the relationship between knowledge and subjectivity, i.e., self-conscious awareness. A central assumption is that knowledge is not produced only by experts. The deconstruction of boundaries between traditional knowledge and power has raised new questions that suggest different ways of knowledge construction representing different worldviews. For example, student experiences and their historical, social, and cultural conditions must be viewed as primary sources of knowledge if they are to be subjects, and involved in the productive educational process. By rejecting metanarratives and universalistic theories—which are from the Eurocentric male, middle class perspective—and by asserting the contextual nature of knowledge and the plurality of meanings, they broaden the base to include marginalized groups and expand knowledge about themselves and their world. This challenges the validity of Eurocentric knowledge "as the exclusive referent for judging what constitutes historical, cultural, and political truth." It asserts that "there is no tradition or story that can speak with authority and certainty for all of humanity" (Giroux, 1991, p. 231).

Schools promote specific notions of knowledge and power by rewarding specific forms of behaviour. School knowledge is influenced by structures of economic/social class power, notions, and assumptions about race, and differences on the basis of gender (Apple, 1999, 2000). When knowledge is politically based, historically embedded, and socially constructed, and therefore subjective (Banks, 1997), then questions that involve the validity of what constitutes acceptable knowledge arise. The social location of those who produce school knowledge and use it as a neutral object to be transmitted to subjects who have different social locations (Freire, 2000[1970]), in combination with the politics of location (Rich, 1986), have brought into focus the relations of power resulting in injustice that underlie these politics. Moreover, the recognition that school knowledge is far from neutral provides a significant explanation as to how it serves students of different groups unequally. If knowledge and power are inextricably linked, then in order to empower students, attention must be paid to the ways in which students acquire knowledge and are given the opportunity to construct, analyze, and deconstruct knowledge to uncover the values and assumptions of curriculum canons or precepts.

THE POLITICS OF DIFFERENCE

Audre Lorde's (1984) point that it is not the differences in themselves, but the social construction and conceptualization of these differences that divide people has, even after so many years, a powerful theoretical and practical resonance. Power relations invariably denote oppressive consequences, whether conscious (and obvious) or not. Those who are different become the other, and their histories, cultures, and experiences are denigrated and/or eradicated. In the literature of postmodern thought, Jacques Derrida (1973) coined the neologism *différance* to imply the unheard and abstract element in conceptualizing difference, because the *a* in differance is only seen and not heard.

From a straightforward definitional perspective, the Oxford Dictionary defines *difference* as "that which distinguishes one thing from another." Difference is a comparative term; it is relational and it is created. The creation of the other implies deviance from the norm—in standards of excellence, achievement, and evaluation. Giroux writes that "to take up the issue of difference is to recognize that it cannot be analyzed unproblematically" (1992, p. 171). The idea of difference as such hides its profoundly political aspect that results in prejudice (the attitude) and discrimination (the behaviour). For those who are different, their inability to challenge these interpretations (their silence and powerlessness) oppresses them. It violates their sense of worth, self-esteem, and overall individual and social identities. The fear of difference is perhaps the greatest impediment to understanding among different people because it creates barriers. Further, it puts the onus on those who are different to cross the distance between their realities and the dominant consciousness, while those who represent the norm avoid their responsibility.

These issues indicate that not only is there a diversity of meaning of the concept of difference, but also that this meaning is not fixed in time and place. Here, difference is taken as a process of construction of meanings in the interplay of power and identity, which brings together groups on the basis of their subordination. It recognizes differences both within and between groups. Democracy implies that despite differences, human beings have equal dignity, and therefore equal rights. Although there is still controversy as to the extent of rights, especially in the economic sphere (due to the inability of many nations to provide those rights), there is a global consensus on basic rights for all (citizenship and voting rights). Education, for example, is considered a basic right, even when the majority of non-industrialized countries are unable to provide education for all.

THE POLITICS OF RECOGNITION

The paradox is that democracy entails universal acceptance of equal dignity on one level (notwithstanding differences), but recognition of individual identity on another (acknowledging differences). As such, democracy signifies recognition. In his seminal essay "The Politics of Recognition," Charles Taylor (1994) defines identity as a person's understanding of who she or he is, of her/his fundamental defining characteristics as a human being. And how one defines oneself is partly dependent on the recognition, misrecognition, or absence of recognition by others. As Taylor notes, non-recognition and/or misrecognition can inflict harm, and literally constitute a form of oppression that incarcerates people in a false, deformed, and existentially reduced mode of being.

Contemporary conceptions of identity are also influenced by postmodernist/poststructuralist writers who seek to deconstruct what they call the logic of identity in Western philosophical and theoretical discourse. The logic of identity conceptualizes objects as measurable (unity and substance) rather than as process. Earlier discussions of identity were located in the area of personality. Social identity research challenged this individualistic frame and subjective definition of the notion of identity as a stabilized factor, an essential personality trait. Identity is no longer seen as a static, unitary trait; nor is it merely a result of socialization. People construct their identities within the social framework. Identity is now seen as being formed in social processes, and in terms of relations because human beings are always in the making. As such, identities are constantly shifting and renegotiable, and the search for new or modified identities, even in places historically largely Anglo-Saxon, such as North America, is continuous.

In terms of difference, then, questions arise. Different from what? Different in what way? And, perhaps more importantly, different from whom? The operative concepts in theorizing difference are both power and identity. The answer to the first question—different from what—requires a definition of the norm, or dominant groups who enjoy dominance over others and are the repositories of power. Those who are not from the norm are different, and this in itself may be the underlying factor for discrimination. Likewise, those who are from the working class suffer from classism, and females are exposed to sexism. As Gilroy (1990) keenly pointed out, these categories stand for hierarchies, and not difference. The concept of power is implicit in the terms racism, classism, and sexism; a domination of white over black; middle class over working class; male over female. The relational equation, then, is that of power. The educational project must be to expose and uncover the patterns of power relations and inequalities.

The second question—different in what way—brings issues of identity of the other into the portrayal of the category of otherness. Those who are different (they; the outsiders) are defined by the dominant group (we; the insiders). Both we and they are artificially constructed in unitary fashion, disregarding the differences within each construct. The physical and economic differences that are used to categorize groups and define people also reproduce inequalities through relations of domination and subordination. The pedagogical issue is the social and historical construction of identity, which is in flux. Essentially, racial, ethnic, gender, and class differences are as irrelevant to the educational process as are the size and shape of students.

Finally, different from whom? By remaining invisible—because whites do not give themselves a racial identity—the dominant group remains outside the hierarchy of social relations, and in that way is not part of the politics of difference. Its supremacy in the ladder of power is ensured (Carby, 1992), while relegating a subaltern status to the other. Pedagogically, the issue is how the historical and social constructions of whiteness and difference are learned. More critically, what opportunities are given to students to deconstruct these conceptions as implying reality? In pedagogical terms, the object is to discern how students "learn to identify, challenge, and rewrite such representations" (Giroux, 1993, p. 21).

Difference, as a historical and social idea, has a long history in the West, and can be traced back to the Enlightenment. From that perspective, human differences are simplistically seen in binary oppositions: difference/sameness, we/them; white/black, male/female, middle class/working class; good/bad, superior/inferior, strong/weak. Binary oppositions were used by conservative theorists to justify inequality and discrimination by associating difference with deficiency and deviance. Liberals recognized difference but avoided the issue, and were blind to the unequal power relations and institutional discrimination that accompanied the conceptions of difference. The other was conceived as static and made peripheral by the domination of a unified norm. Radical theorists focus on the changing social construction of difference and identity and their multiplicity.

The concept of difference has also been the focus of feminist theories in the West. Initially, this was in defence of their difference as women from men in a patriarchal society. More recently, it has focused on the differences among women, specifically between privileged white middle class women and the disadvantaged working class and/or ethnic minority women. Minority feminist scholars, as discussed above, have pointed out how the experiences of minority women differ from those of white women: not only are they subjected to two forms of oppression (sexism and racism), but the combination of the two makes it different, and not simply more acute. The multiple instances and levels of oppression may induce what Carty (1991) and Mohanty (1995) have called multi-layered platforms of marginalization in the lives of non-European women. Not to recognize this difference in experiences is to deny the difference in the sexism that black and white women experience, and the racism that men and women encounter.

These conceptualizations and their possible pragmatics create very real discrepancies for those who are different in terms of race, sex and class. The salient point is that the dominant group and minority groups (racial, ethnic, class, or gender) have very different conceptions of how difference works. Dominant group responses to differences may vary in several ways, including silence, guilt, and fear. It is the refusal to recognize the effects of distorted connotations given to differences, therefore, that has to cease (see Hartman, 1997). As such, Stuart Hall would still be right:

> Identities are a matter of "becoming" as well as of "being" .... Far from being eternally fixed in some essentialised past, they are subject to the continuous "play" of history, culture and power .... Identities are the names we give to the different ways we are positioned by, and position ourselves within, the narratives of the past (Hall, 1990, p. 225).

Identity is formed along multiple axes that include, among others, race, gender, and social class. Identity surfaces at the individual level, but each person has many social identities (such as ethnic, sexual, and class identities) that develop meaning in people's lives both at the ideological/political and social/cultural levels. People's multiple identities are not apparent in all contexts, and represent different spheres of reality in everyday life. Different ones are important at different times. Generally, what people define as "real" are real in their consequences, and reality is defined socially by individuals and groups of individuals who serve as definers of reality.

At the individual level, those who identify with a group can redefine the meaning and norms of group identity. Individual and collective identities are constructed in three areas: the biological, the social and the cultural (Aronowitz, 1992). Our biological attributes—gender, race, and ethnicity—become meaningful and are defined in our interactions with people. While gender, race, and ethnic identities are ascribed and cannot usually be changed, class position, which is also assigned at birth, can be changed. The given characteristics do not have meaning in themselves, but become defining factors. Identity is, therefore, constructed relationally.

Cultural identities are a "conjuncture of our past with the social, cultural and economic relations we live within" (Rutherford, 1990, p.

19). Although we may be a précis of the past (Gramsci, 1988), our cultural identities are not fixed. Identity is a constructed sense of self that also incorporates views of self-help by others. Identity is influenced by one's location in relation to others and the way others identify and define us. It is influenced by the dilemma of differences (Minow, 1990) and by the notion of different degrees of othering (Mercer, 1992). In this construction, schools play a significant role in reproducing racial, gender, and class differences.

Culture

Culture refers to the way in which a group of people responds to the environment in terms of cognition, emotion and behaviour. In that sense, "culture is ... excerpted by human thought from ... world history, and invested with sense and meaning" (Hartman, 1997, p. 27). Culture, therefore, is a dynamic rather than a static phenomenon. Despite being bound up with the most fundamental epistemological questions, the issue of culture has been considered superfluous within the economic and political challenges of daily life. If culture is a way of seeing the world, and if seeing the world has any relevance to changing the world, then it would be necessary to understand effectively and respond pragmatically to issues that concern the way in which we see the world. The purpose of multicultural education is to create new possibilities in confronting the ways in which we see the world. Culture plays a significant role in production and reproduction in schools. Cultural struggle is essential to political and economic struggle. Multiculturalism represents that cultural struggle.

Moreover, formations of difference, whether in schools or in the generalized, societal interactions of people, are now influenced by rapidly emerging global constructions of culture. Here, as globalization affects all aspects of people's lives, the mediating of difference and related issues that are undertaken in schools will have to deal with the homogenizing forces of global media and information technology that are incessantly shaping the way learners, teachers, and others define, operationalize, and eventually manage or problematize difference. The irony in this is that while globalization is supposedly opening up the world's cultures and differences to one another, by default and primarily via the hegemonic cultural forces of its major sponsors, it is actually indirectly advancing the Westernization of the world. In this regard, the role of education and educators to welcome and sustain multi-centric notions of culture and difference cannot be overestimated.

The emergence of the discourses of the new politics of cultural difference in the social sciences has important implications for redefining diverse conceptions of culture. Culture here signifies special ways in which particular classes and social groups live and make sense out of the world and their life situations. As such, the concept of culture is directly related to how people's relations are structured in terms of the differences discussed above, and selectively explains the discrepancies that arise in defining and using the practices of knowledge and experience.

In modernist discourse, culture is an organizing principle, which homogenizes and creates borders around ethnicity, class, and gender, despite its emphasis on democratic ideals. However, neither dominant nor minority cultures are homogenous. Individuals see the world from their own perspectives and have multiple consciousness. The politics of location, as Rich (1986) and Bhabha (1994) have discussed, explains how people are grounded and confined because they are located unequally in terms of race, ethnicity, class, and gender. Multicultural connotes numerous cultures. Cultural aspects based on biological differences of race and ethnicity are the ones most obviously perceived. However, gender differences are cultural too, and these are also constructed around biological differences.

The notion of multiculturalism is closely related to the concepts of race and ethnicity. The question of hierarchy in categories of oppression leads to the view that issues are often different for different groups, and the impact is weakened when dealt with simultaneously. Yet everyone is a member of some racial or ethnic group, and of other groups simultaneously. Discrimination based on perception of difference is the problem. And multiculturalism speaks about and advances the right to difference (Ghosh, 1996). Here, the need is to question structures and patterns of relationships, not to prioritize groups. Instead of giving credibility to the current limited interpretation of multiculturalism, it is the commonality and intersection of experiences in terms of race and ethnicity, class and gender, which we need to understand.

Women, for example, may manifest differences in thought processes that correspond to their difference in status and lack of power in society. It would be possible that all knowledge is gendered, classed, and culture-based. The concept of multiculturalism must contain within it all these cultures because the effects of their social definition and construction are similar. The end result is that the segregation of populations is eliminated. The root factors innate within the concept are political, thinly concealing the twin facets of dominance and exclusivity, and symbolizing some kind of primeval power struggle (Goldberg, 1992). Multiculturalism must challenge both marginalization and incorporation by recognizing disadvantage as intersecting with class, colour, gender, and culture, and as being embedded in history.

The challenge to the dominant Eurocentric domination that "colonizes definitions of the normal" (Giroux, 1991, p. 225) is central to multicultural philosophy. That challenge comes as much from racial and ethnic groups as from women and the working class. Each of these groups is identified by their particular culture, but they often converge to make individual and group experiences complex and multiple. Linking the experiences of minority groups, and making connections between different experiences enables recognition of similarities and variations.

Dominant Group

Multiculturalism is a controversial issue, and hotly debated at the educational level. This implies that it is an arena of power struggles, where different constituencies are struggling with their different interests. One problem with the notion of existing concepts of multiculturalism has been its almost exclusive concern with the other. It has failed to question the norm of whiteness and the domination of white culture by being invisible. By remaining concealed, and removing the dominant group from race and/or ethnicity, the focus on difference is depoliticized. Thus, asymmetrical relations of power are maintained. Subordinate groups do not own the categories of race, gender, and class. Surely the dominant or majority groups belong to some race if Homo sapiens are to be categorized. They must also have gender and class affiliations. Race, gender, and class categories have been socially constructed by dominant discourse and practice to determine the social location of the other; multiculturalism, in its present form, does not challenge the dominant group's understanding of the world (Carty, 1991). Yet it is the very encounter with the dominant group that produces the subordinate groups; "the marginal [is] a consequence of the authority invested in the centre" (Julien and Mercer, 1988, p. 3). Multiculturalism must conceptualize issues of race and ethnicity, gender and class as part of a wider discourse on power and powerlessness, not only the latter. The dominant group must be a part of the multicultural ideology because it has to take part of the responsibility for the emerging socio-cultural conditions, which threaten democracy and global stability. For the dominant group, multiculturalism must be "the desire to extend the reference of 'us' as far as we can" (Rorty, 1991, p. 23) if democracy is to have any meaning.

Fusion of Cultures

Our future survival as human beings in the face of global human and environmental problems is contingent upon interdependence. We must develop the ability to relate within a framework of equality, which involves an ameliorated vision of our future. Multiculturalism must analyze the meaning of race and ethnicity, gender, and class as social and historical constructs that involve all citizens of a democracy, both dominant and subordinate. Difference is "a dynamic human force, one which is enriching rather than threatening to the defined self, when there are shared goals" (Lorde, 1984, p. 45). Multiculturalism involves majority and minority groups alike, and must formulate new goals in a new paradigm where definitions of power enable relating across differences. In the new terrains of social comportment among previously disjointed groups, "commitments to cultural diversity [anticipate] ... accommodation, integration and transformation" (Goldberg, 1994, p. 7). These should all enhance the global interdependence that is now becoming a universal fact of life.

Multiculturalism as such refers, therefore, to a community in the making and not to a plurality of cultures. Its meaning encompasses the creation of spaces within which different communities (defined by race/ethnicity, gender, and/or class) feel encouraged and are able to grow. The creation of public spaces enables interaction. In this genre and possible action, the construction of a syncretic culture is characterized by consensus while maintaining separate identities. Postmodern thought resists the idea of culture as an organizing principle, which creates borders around ethnicity, class, and gender. Creating borders homogenizes cultures within a culture, although neither dominant nor minority cultures are homogeneous. Taylor (1994) points out that we cannot judge other cultures, for a culture that sufficiently diverges from the norm would speak about, and stand for, situations that constitute different historical and life possibilities for people in different locations, conditions, and relationships. So, what has to happen is a fusion of horizons (a term Taylor borrows from Gadamer), which involves a broader horizon in which we negotiate what Homi Bhabha calls the third space (Bhabha, 1994). This means developing new ideas and vocabularies, which will enable us to make the comparisons partly through transforming our own standards. To do that effectively, three points need to be made:

- The third space is not an extension of established values; it is rather a renegotiation of cultural space. Interpreting one level of experience and transposing that to another is creating a multidimensional condition. The words *syncretic* and *hybridity* are useful to imply culture as process. Syncretic suggests the union of opposite principles and practices, while hybridity means to create and innovate by articulating a new way. The third space offers the opportunity to create conventions and practices within and between different modes of meaning. It is the harmonization of cultures, not their dissolution, disappearance, or disintegration.

- The fusion of cultures does not imply difference-blindness, which is neither desirable nor possible. Human beings are different from each other in various ways, and this does not translate into deficiency or deviance when they differ from a traditional norm. It simply means that they are different, but also that they have the right to be different. Indeed, the validation of their cultural, social, and gender differences, and the development of their individual identities, should be a focus of multicultural education. The aim of multicultural education is thus to empower all students with an ethical and democratic vision of society within which they can make a variety of contributions appropriate to their talents, needs, and aspirations.

- Fusion does not mean homogenization; rather, it emphasizes identity because individuals see the world from their own perspectives and have multiple identities, some of which may be contradictory. This makes their experiences dialectical. An example is being bilingual or multilingual. We do not forget one language when we speak another; rather, we are enriched by the knowledge of the other. Diversity will diminish in importance not because we will be the same but because it is natural.

IMPLICATIONS FOR EDUCATION

Crisis in Epistemology

The questions arising from the evolution of the concept of knowledge and the function of schooling are central to the teaching profession. What kinds of knowledge will best ensure that students are critical and participating citizens? Who produces school knowledge, and who speaks for society? How are the various groups of students socially and culturally located in terms of the socio-cultural point of view of school knowledge: the curriculum? Does the curriculum serve students differently depending upon their gender, race, ethnic, and class differences? Do teachers assume that their pedagogical practices are suitable for all students even though there are differences in ways of knowing and learning?

These questions transform the process of teaching. They focus on the relation between discursive practices and the practical subjectivity of those who produce and/or consume them. They also change the student-teacher equation where, as Freire (2000) pointed out, knowledge is not an object to be transmitted from the teacher who has it to the students who do not. Knowledge is seen increasingly as resulting from specific social and historical relations, rather than as static entities that are context and value-free. As such, students are active knowers at the centre of the learning process, knowing subjects, rather than at the receiving end acquiring knowledge as objects. The changes in curriculum content and process implied by the major shifts challenge the knowledge taught by schools as the only legitimate form of learning. The politics of location become central to the teaching and learning act. Conventional teaching practices and knowledge are, therefore, at stake.

These challenges to traditional pedagogy confront all societies, but they are particularly crucial in multicultural societies where the complex needs of students with cultural differences are usually ignored. Critical pedagogy focuses attention on culturally determined content and practices, and provides the basic framework for multicultural pedagogy. In the multicultural arrangements of learning, therefore, "students must develop multicultural literacy and cross-cultural competency if they are to become knowledgeable, reflective, and caring citizens in the twenty-first century" (Banks, 1997, p. 13).

Multiculturalism as a philosophy must be translated into education. Lived realities cannot be expressed without formal mediation. While realities are always mediated, the need for radical transformation involves how people view their specific situations and needs, i.e., from the assimilationist mode of traditional education rooted in conservative theories (the monocultural), and the accommodation of pluralist theories, to the multicultural mode of critical pedagogy (the heterogeneous). This change must be transformative, not incremental. Transformative change is radical because it is a change in view, perspective, and methodology. It alters the relationship between teacher and student, and between student and the learning environment. It is characterized by a paradigm switch, and thus internally generated, not externally controlled.

Education and the Politics of Difference and Recognition

The cultural pluralist approach to multicultural education by those who consider themselves liberal is additive, and the focus is upon culture as exotic. Education that addresses the needs of a multicultural society deals with social inequalities and inequities, and links power and empowerment with race, gender, and class (among other social constructions) for social change. It attempts to close we/they dichotomies, which maintain inequality. It challenges the prevailing understanding of the process of knowledge generation of Eurocentric subjugated knowledges.

Knowledge is directly tied to people's differences, because it locates and situates them in relation to the dominant group in terms of race and ethnicity, gender, and class. The central issue is not merely acknowledging difference (Mohanty, 1990). Multicultural education should enable us to express our differences in other ways (Lewis, 1990), going beyond the equality concept that remains within the existing traditional structure, to a configuration that would encompass differences. Schools need to legitimize multiple traditions of knowledge. And to do that inclusively, multicultural education must address issues to the politics of difference, not just descriptively furnish the components of plurality that will only highlight difference per se.

A significant aspect of multicultural education is to teach dominant groups to challenge oppression, especially because their privileged position tends to make it difficult for them to see the world critically. Multicultural education is for *all* students and *all* teachers, not only for oppressed groups. However, equal treatment implies that because all students are not on a level playing field, schools need to give the marginalized students situation-specific treatment that is primarily designed to level the uneven historical and current appropriations in resources, skills, and achievements. As a philosophy, it needs to permeate the school culture, in order for all students to be empowered to cope with existing realities, and have a vision for the future. In the final analysis, it is what Freire (1985) has called education for critical consciousness that could deploy new programs of learning that may furnish novel and hopefully effective strategies and practices for liberation. Again, the persistence of educational, and therefore socio-economic, inequities, especially in Western multicul-

tural societies, is creating some doubt in the minds of critical pedagogy educators, who urgently call for the pragmatic operationaliza-
tion and not just the academic discussion of the project to achieve the
still-evasive forums of equity and development for all. In this regard,
McLaren (1998, p. 452) writes:

> The critical pedagogy to which I am referring needs to be made less
> in-formative and more per-formative, less a pedagogy directed
> toward the interrogation of written texts than a corporeal pedagogy
> grounded in the lived experiences of students. Critical pedagogy, as
> I am revisioning it from a Marxist perspective, is a pedagogy that
> brushes against the grain of textual foundationalism, ocular
> fetishism, and the monumentalist abstraction of theory that char-
> acterizes most critical practice within teacher education classrooms.
> I am calling for a pedagogy in which a revolutionary multicultural
> ethics is performed—is lived in the streets—rather than simply
> reduced to the practice of reading texts (although the reading of
> texts with other texts, against other texts, and upon other texts is
> decidedly an important exercise). Teachers need to build upon the
> textual politics that dominates most multicultural classrooms by
> engaging in a politics of bodily and affective investment, which
> means "walking the talk," and working in those very communities
> one purports to serve.

If and when we decide to achieve McLaren's recommendations, as
well as other suggestions that could be contextually effective, then
the implications of power differentials must be comprehensively
examined. Here, one can see that in order to aim for a practically
functioning and situation-changing pedagogy, one must critically
develop a relentless program of understanding the enduring but still
malleable contours of the social and historical construction of difference that is, somehow, still succeeding in devaluing and excluding

the knowledge, and as dangerously, the contemporary realities of the other. The question then should involve how schools organize differences in social and pedagogical interactions that influence the way in which teachers and students define themselves and each other. In Harstock's earlier but still relevant question, does the school "construct an understanding of the world that is sensitive to difference" (Harstock, 1987, p. 189)?

Schools, generally speaking, not only sustain asymmetrical social relations of power, but foster the binary oppositions in society by confirming that the primary term (the "white" in white/black; the "male" in male/female) is superior. Students are socialized to react to human differences in diverse ways: with dislike and fear (racism); with the option of disregarding differences (consensus theories), of accommodating them (liberal theories), or incorporating them (critical multiculturalism). Differences have been used to separate and create walls, rather than to be related across on an equal basis. Those who are different become the other, and their histories, cultures, and experiences are disparaged and/or obliterated and effaced (for example, Native populations in North America and colonized cultures around the world). Pedagogy must be developed around the politics of difference in order to cross borders, not construct barriers. This suggests transcending boundaries of language, culture, and perspectives. Welch (1991) recommended several ways to do this. First, the learning process must represent the construction of subjectivities and identities that link experiences of the other to school curriculum and practices. Race, ethnicity, gender, and class experiences combine to shape identity in complex and contradictory ways.

Secondly, the historical differences that manifest themselves as ideologies such as racism, sexism, and classism need to be dealt with, in order to reveal how asymmetrical power relations create different conditions for different groups and individuals. Furthermore, the ways in which differences within and between groups result in social hierarchy through school structures need to be understood. The idea is to construct knowledge in which multiple voices and worldviews are legitimized so that new patterns of relating are forged. It is essential for both insider and outsider to understand the politics of difference. It is especially important for the different to be allowed to define themselves: "It is axiomatic," says Audre Lorde (1984), "that if we do not define ourselves for ourselves, we will be defined by others—for their use and to our detriment" (p. 45). Finally, the creative function of difference needs to be recognized so that it can become the strength necessary for interdependence: "Difference is that raw and powerful connection from which our personal power is forged" (Lorde, 1984, p. 112).

Children's experiences and identities are constructed in relation to their gender, class, and race, as well as their ethnicity (which is mediated by culture) and their location in history. For example, children of immigrant parents are not what their parents are or were because of their positional identities in history and culture. The question, then, is how educators can facilitate students' attempts at making sense of the self and the other in the process of empowerment.

The differences in cultural content of children result in differences in communication and interaction styles, as well as cognitive and learning styles. This makes it necessary for the teacher, as mediator in the education process, to develop a knowledge base on which to build understanding. Knowledge of students is imperative if teachers are to guide their learning experiences, and lead students to see the connections between what is learned in school and their lived experiences. Education is not merely collecting disjointed knowledge; rather, it is acquiring conceptual schemes. Learning is to connect, to make meaning, and must be built on students' experiences and what they know. It behooves us as educators to understand student experiences, and how identities are produced differently. Only then can teachers provide students with the analytical tools to deal with problems of unresolved identities and challenge experiences of racism, sexism, and other inequities.

The effect of difference on identity is one's location in relation to others, and more importantly, how that location produces a concept of self in relation to the way others identify and define us. As Hall (1997, p. 174) notes, "[for example] to be English is to know yourself in relation to the French, to the hot-blooded Mediterraneans, and to the passionate, traumatized Russian soul. You know that you are what everybody else on the globe is not." In these constructions of identity, schools play a significant role in perpetuating racial, gender, and class differences. The dynamics of identity and identification in modern society are complex. The daily experiences that shape the identities of minority group students, the psychosocial impact of prejudice, and discrimination based on race and ethnicity, gender, and class, are of great significance, especially with increasing ethnic and racial tensions in schools and society. Key questions relate to the implications of identity for self-esteem and school achievement, and of ethnic identity for integration and relationship to the dominant culture. The development of oppositional identities is a rejection of the dominant culture, knowledge, and norms by some minority group students.

To incorporate the transformative change, we must redefine multicultural education as radically different from an apolitical representation of education that views culture as artifact, which emphasizes difference but nonetheless attempts to provide strategies to accommodate these differences through equity policies within the dominant traditional structure. It does not change the situation of sexism, racism, and classism in society. It is this that prevents people with differences from maximizing their potential. It places them unfairly and invisibly in a supposedly democratic society. Multicultural education must recognize the politics of difference and culture, and capitalize on the potential offered by difference to develop it as a creative force rather than treat it as a deficiency.

CONCLUSION

How we come to know, and what we know, defines our position in the world. In their present framework, multicultural educational programs generally emphasize pluralism and benign versions of culture as artifact. This has become part of the problem and discourages change. These programs do not address the real problematic of the politics of difference, power, and dominant hegemony. They remain ineffective because the focus is on addressing the other: those who do not belong to mainstream culture. When the salient issues are not addressed, the inequalities in society are perpetuated. The current levels of racism, sexism, and class discrimination stand witness to the failure of multicultural education to lead students to an understanding of the possibilities of an integrated, rather than a segregated, society.

It is obvious that an educational model of assimilation, which serves the needs of a monocultural society, cannot provide equal opportunity to all groups. The change to a recast multicultural model implies a dramatic shift in worldview, a paradigm shift. However, because this has not been recognized as such, multicultural education has failed to achieve its true objectives due to a paradigm blindness. As Edelsky (1990) pointed out, paradigm blindness is not politically innocent.

"The contemporary search for educational choices is a reflection of the tensions between a changing social reality and an inherited system held captive by its past" (Singh, 1992, p. 12). Traditional theorists have ignored the structural causes of inequality, negated the importance of identity (racial, ethnic, cultural, class, and gender) and blamed the victim for failure. Radical theorists have emphasized the political aspects of schooling because of its functions of reproduction and legitimization of the dominant culture. The theoretical advances made by radical theorists provide valuable insights in explaining the means by which inequality for difference is perpetuated through the content (explicit and implicit), process, and psychological dimensions of an unfair school system.

Critical pedagogy enables an analysis of the dialectics of consciousness and cultural domination by race, class, and gender. Given the nature and magnitude of changes in society, a new kind of education to create a better future is imperative. Students who are different must be seen in a new light in a system that has hitherto excluded and marginalized them. A major problem with the federal Multicultural Policy is that it cannot be effectively implemented in education because education is a provincial responsibility, and neither legal nor political remedies are available in the absence of a substantive rights guarantee. The legal provisions (or protections) to prevent discrimination on grounds of ethnicity or race in the Charter of Rights and Freedoms have implications for education. It is significant, however, that the Multiculturalism clause for education is vague. It is true that the Canadian federal government assists multicultural programs and research in education through a department (originally set up as a Multiculturalism Directorate in 1972 under the Secretary of State). But the lack of federal control over education, and provincial legislation in general, has limited federal ability to influence education in this direction to any meaningful degree.

Across the country, multiculturalism has been variously interpreted in education. Notwithstanding the fact that Canada is an immigrant country, the provincial departments of education have historically maintained a policy of assimilation. The education of various groups in Canada has been assimilationist towards an Anglo-dominated culture, although at least a quarter of the population has been French and concentrated in Quebec. Furthermore, the country was built by immigrants from Europe and the Third World. Following consensus theories, education's role was seen as cultural transmission in the process of human capital formation, and therefore essential for developing Canada. Within the vision of a monocultural society, it implied non-recognition or non-acceptance of cultural differences (except for the dominant English and the subordinate French) for ethnic group relations in all of Canada, including Quebec. Racial and ethnic (as well as gender and class) differences were negated in an attempt to devalue non-dominant group characteristics. The exclusion of the other was structural. To achieve more inclusive and effective notions and practices of multiculturalism, the role of multicultural education becomes paramount. And this paramountcy is again elevated by the reality of the globalization of difference (discussed in chapter four) that should force us not only to share spaces of schooling, but also to coexist, peacefully and productively, in multi-ethnic, multi-racial, and multi-linguistic locations of work and residency. In the next chapter, select and topic-specific discussions of multicultural education are presented and analyzed.

2 | ISSUES IN MULTICULTURAL EDUCATION

I do not want my house to be walled in on all sides and my windows to be stuffed.
I want the cultures of all lands to be blown about my house as freely as possible.
But I refuse to be blown off my feet by any.

—*Mahatma Gandhi*

Since its inception, evolution has been the key element in the various developmental phases of Canada's education policy. However, the most recent of those, multiculturalism, as an ideology or worldview, makes a radical departure from earlier approaches such as assimilation. This is so because, despite being within the traditional model of consensus, its liberal rhetoric implies equal opportunity to all ethnic groups by giving equal status to all cultures. However, the modern democratic view of the world in the policy of multiculturalism ignores ethnic, racial, and socio-economic differences. It legitimizes a Eurocentric view of the world with other cultures, and depoliticizes culture. It is not surprising that multicultural education began with an emphasis on culture as exotic and as artifact. The song and dance routine completely depoliticized culture, and avoided issues of discrimination and race relations. It also absolved educators for neglecting other cultures as long as they were willing to observe psychologically soothing but otherwise ineffective multicultural days and festivities.

In its not-yet-attained pragmatic perspective, multicultural education aims to provide a learning environment devoid of the painful experiences of discrimination and inequality. The rising interest in multicultural education, however, does not ensure its effectiveness. To be effective in removing discrimination, educational programs must be founded on a philosophy of education linked to equity and empowerment. For educators, this involves an understanding of the construction of difference and inequity created around conceptions of race and ethnicity, gender, and class, among other things. This comprises knowledge of, and sensitivity to, the social consequences of difference expressed through prejudice, and discrimination in the form of racism, sexism, and classism. The pedagogical concepts that are involved here are identity and empowerment.

As educators, we must not only be spurred by equality legislation, but also motivated by principles of justice (Darling-Hammond, 2002) and by the moral and ethical imperatives of caring. The question arises as to whether there is a conflict between our moral commitment to equity, and our pursuit of excellence as educators. This chapter begins with the query, is equity-based, quality education possible? Equity, in this sense, and as discussed in the previous chapter, connotes more than the measurable equalization of expenditure and results; it also incorporates the equitable representation of histories, cultures, and even expectations in the design, implementation, and evaluation of the education system.

Equity, Quality, and Education

The cornerstone of a modern, democratic society is equity. Equity and justice are complementary concepts that go hand in hand. Equity of educational opportunity in current democracies is regarded as one of the most important means of achieving a just society. Societies aiming at social equality and economic justice have made public education available to those groups that, due to discrimination, were at one time deprived of this facility: the poor, women, and racial/ethnic minority groups among others. The educational aim of a democratic society is to produce fully enfranchised citizens, no matter what their social, economic, and ethnocultural origins. Public education, therefore, must be both equitable and excellent, with educators committing themselves to quality education for all children (Bang, 2002; Ruiz, 2002).

Educational reformers continue to intensely debate the issues of equity of opportunity, and the search for quality in various aspects of the system. Unfortunately, policy-makers have created a false dichotomy between equity and quality, and have often aimed at achieving one at the expense of the other. The view that quality and equity are antithetical is based on a misconception of the two terms. Conservative theorists related equity in education to compensatory programs for the special needs and disabilities of marginalized groups. The dominant groups were identified with programs of excellence which, it was assumed, the other groups could not achieve. Based on that perspective, equity and quality have been misconstructed as being at polar ends of a continuum.

Equity is aimed at eliminating discrimination, and achieving, relatively speaking, a just society. The ideas of *liberté* and *égalité,* as they are operationalized in the Western tradition, emanated from the French Revolution. They are basic to the constitutional provisions of many modern democracies. The doctrine of equality of persons is related to the concept of justice. The legal theory of justice derives from John Rawls' *A Theory of Justice* (1971), in which he provides two principles. The first is that all citizens have the same claim to equal basic liberties. The second is that social and economic inequalities must satisfy two conditions: the equality of opportunity principle, which implies that all positions are open to every person (the fairness concept); and the difference principle, which means that the greatest benefit must go to the least advantaged members of society (the equity concept). As such, the comprehensive notion of equity would advance the recognition of difference in educational and other settings and influence how we relate to the basic conceptions of social responsibility. As a social institution, education is equally concerned with both principles: equity of opportunity, and the difference precept. The latter has been very controversial in education because it means that there can be affirmative action, such as special provisions for groups that have historically suffered discrimination. It is assumed that these special provisions may include lower standards of achievement for entry into courses or programs, and even jobs, for disadvantaged groups whose historical oppression has resulted in lower status and educational achievement.

While most would associate the current debates and provisions of affirmative action with the United States, the idea and its practice actually started in India (where it is called positive discrimination) and, as in the US, has also been controversial there. In Canada, equity policy in jobs for women, visible minorities, Native groups, and disabled people is somewhat different because it gives preference to people from the targeted groups *when qualifications are similar*. A rebuttal to critics of the equity policy is that historically, a preference for male candidates of the dominant group has been in practice without a written policy, even when they have been less qualified. So the current equity policy in Canada, instead of focusing on the historical core of inequity, assumes *a priori* the existence of a level playing field. That, of course, is not the case, as white males have already been given all the possibilities for acquiring the necessary educational skills. That is complemented by these groups' incorporation into a kind of socio-economic and political relationship that is already controlled by those who emotionally, culturally, and, of course, family-wise, identify with them, and therefore are apparently and expectedly sensitive to their needs and desires. Hence, the need, not necessarily for a quota-based affirmative action program, but at least a more historically inclusive notion of the equity policy so as to achieve a more rational platform for the perennially elusive level playing field.

In education, equity is seen from three aspects: equality of opportunity to achieve certain goals; equality of condition; and equality of outcome, or results. Radical educational theorists have argued that equity of opportunity is meaningless to children when they come from unequal conditions, with unequal cultural capital. Schools actually reinforce existing inequalities when they do not allow for social differences that affect learning and achievement. Moreover, because both educational institutions and teachers could lack the all-too-important intercultural competence (Bennett, 1999), different students are not treated equally in a system that perpetuates the dominant culture, values, and norms through the curriculum and organization, and with which learners cannot identify. If the ultimate aim is social equality, i.e., equity in the sense that all opportunities are equally accessible regardless of accidents of birth or difference, then the focus must be on educational outcomes.

Equity does not connote sameness or evenness: it means fairness and implies justice. As such, the process involves giving special treatment and opportunities (which are not necessarily the same thing) to those who have special or different needs. In that vein, the idea of equity, especially from the perspective of educators, must involve "the passion [to] continually develop the skills to teach ALL students" (Ruiz, 2002, p. 192) so that they are empowered to make life choices that are transformative in both their individual and social possibilities. In this context, the construct of quality implies the degree of excellence. Both terms—quality and excellence—signify a comparison, either in contrast to a normal group (norm-referenced) or in relation to some defined criteria (criterion-referenced). The construction of both norm and criterion-referenced excellence are based on the culture, values, and norms defined by the dominant group, and universally applied, despite considerable diversity in students. If, however, quality and excellence are viewed as self-actualisation and self-improvement, then equity and quality converge into equality.

Achieving equity does not, and should not, imply a lowering of standards. Extending access without attention to improving quality is to maintain inequality indirectly. Equality is achieved *only* when quality education is available to *all*. Conversely, improving quality by ignoring diversity in students is to subvert democracy. Excellence in education can be achieved only if all children, the broadest possible range, are allowed to develop their potential. If the aim of education is the empowerment of all students, then the dichotomy in equality and quality disappears. In students' lives, however, there are contradictions between the legal aspect of equality and the reality of inequality. Discrimination based on differences of race and ethnicity, gender and class is a part of the educational experiences of some students. These have serious implications for the life-chances of students, which are their chances of sharing in the social and economic rewards of society. In addition, discrimination makes their daily lives stressful and painful.

Multicultural Policy and Inequity

Despite equality legislation in various Western nations—Britain, the United States, Canada, and Australia—different regimes of discrimination, especially racism, are still present and enduring. Even to the surprise of many Canadians, who may uncritically see their society as caring and comparatively less racist than the United States, a 1993 national poll found that most Canadians have racist attitudes, even if they do not express them publicly (Bergman, 1993). However, a historical comparison of ethnic inequality between 1931 and in Canada, measured in occupational terms, indicates a moderate decline in the significance of ethnicity, which nevertheless continues to exert its influence on occupational achievement (Lautard and Guppy, 1990). Since the multicultural policy has been in effect, its impact on Canadian society would appear to be negligible in terms of affecting inequality. Studies show that in terms of socio-economic status, inequality is more marked among ethnic groups than it is between genders (Lautard and Guppy, 1990). The penetration of ethnic group members into elite groups remains limited, although certain visible minorities are present in a number of professions as well as in higher education, and this may be influenced by immigration patterns (Lessard and Crespo, 1992). Continuously though, gender, class dynamics, race, and ethnicity are relations that underpin the development of Canada as a nation-state. In these social and intercultural dymanics, the socializing function of school is very important. To do this effectively, learning spaces must realize that social integration is not only a personal and individual process, it is also a dialectical process. It involves conflicts in individual identity, in the construction and reconstruction of social relationships, and in the experiences defined by social attributes such as gender, class, ethnicity, and race. Although integration is an individual process, individuals are often perceived as members of a group, and thus stereotyped, rather than perceived on an individual basis.

Construction of Difference

The literature on racism, sexism, and classism has assigned the causes to either individual values and beliefs or to structural inequities in society and its institutions. It is also becoming clear that attention to the dynamics and the contradictions in the inter-relationships of race, gender, and class in everyday life in schools is increasingly being highlighted. The emergence of the simultaneous categorization of race with gender and class makes the relationships complex. In addition, there is the tendency to subsume the categories of race and gender into that of class. It is important to recognize that on the one hand each stands alone, and on the other hand they are interdependent, and this makes the set of relationships very complex. Although race (or ethnicity for that matter) is not "class under another name" (Goldberg, 1992, p. 548), the two are related, in that race, ethnicity, gender, and class are classifications in social positions, and reflect relations of power. While sexism is embedded in the dynamics of race and class relations, racism is interrelated to patriarchy and class. Class is intertwined with gender and race because some women are better off than men in another class. As such, the bifurcated consciousness that sustains the dialectic where the world is divided into such categories would be marred, at least in the long run, by untenable analytical and practical foundations.

The relations are simultaneously, and more than ever, in conflict while being interdependent. However, race, class and sex are not parallel positions: they are qualitatively different. The production of difference, in schools and elsewhere, therefore, implies that race, class, and sex are not additive. That is, the three categories do not make discrimination three times worse. Their combination makes discrimination much worse, but also different depending upon how individuals are positioned in the classroom or school at a certain time. For example, the focus on race is thought to be weakened if gender is dealt with simultaneously. To deal with these issues effectively, the concept as well as the practical possibilities of culture must be revisited. Here, despite its emphasis on democracy, equality, and justice, modernist discourse views culture as an organizing principle that creates borders around race, ethnicity, gender, and class. These borders create inequalities, and the distance between the centres and margins of power are reproduced through the school and other institutions. Race, ethnicity, gender, and class are defining and structuring categories in school as in society.

As analytical categories, race, ethnicity, gender, and class are social constructions. As sociological concepts, they have changed over time, and are not fixed entities even if hegemonic texts would want to believe otherwise (Bhabha, 1994). As systems of classification based on physical characteristics (race and ethnicity), biological character- istics (gender), and economic status (class), there is no evidence of association with mental or behavioural characteristics. The signifi- cant point is that there is as much variance within as between groups in so-called races, and in sexes as well as classes. Moreover, the classi- fications have no relevance either as a basis for assignment of rights, or as grounds for discrimination. The concepts of gender, race, and class indicate changing social relations, and serve to disaggregate populations and form boundaries. Inherently political, because they veil domination and exclusion, they are symbolic of some form of underlying power struggle (Goldberg, 1992). The injuries of racial, gender, and class discrimination are often hidden, but they are nonetheless painful. Students at risk are those who do not make it in the school system, many of whom, for example, are from minority ethnocultural groups, or poor, and/or female. Multicultural educa- tion means ensuring, through the total environment, that school is not a place for hurtful experiences for students simply because they are different. The differences of race and ethnicity, gender and class are characteristics, which are as irrelevant in predicting children's potential as the colour of one's eyes or one's height.

Race

Once more, it should be clear that while the term *race* is being used with few qualifications, the underlying assumption is that race is not a biological fact, and does not represent any constant and/or consis- tent biological categories. Race and the so-called racial characteristics and qualities are, therefore, social constructions that infinitesimally represent the worldview as well as the specific time and space inter- ests of their constructors (Dei, 1996). As many specialists in the area (e.g. biologists) will tell us, there are no races, only racists. From the point of view of molecular biology, one may even find that a group of people in the Congo could have more in common with Swedes than Swedes would have with other Nordic people. Regardless of differences in features and skin colour, Homo sapiens is a homogeneous entity from an objective and scientific point of view. All the same, race, as a concept that differentiates people, has become a living reality within human consciousness. Initially used to justify unequal treatment of colonized peoples, it now refers to meanings constructed around any arbitrary classification of people on the assumption that there are biological and genetic variations.

Race and racism are defining concepts that construct our understanding of Canada as a nation where the "founding races" depicted the norm as white in establishing their relationship with the original peoples and with immigrants. The lack of acknowledgement that racism still exists (even after the demise of colonialism) is largely responsible for the lack of attention to racism in schools and society until very recently. This lack of attention given to the special needs of minority students results in suppressing their potential. The continuities of race and racism also imply that those who benefit from the existence of these categories, i.e., those who achieve livelihood advancements based on their race, would want the full maintenance of the house (metaphorically speaking) that race has initially built for them. But to dismantle the racial house will be anything but easy, for, as Goldberg reminds us in *The Racial State* (2002), it is also government structures in the so-called democratic societies that have been greatly responsible for the maintenance of racial categories as well as for the direct support of some racial groups at the direct expense of other, differently racialized groups.

The contemporary social construction of the term *ethnicity*, on the other hand, implies a shared descent, which may hastily assume a biological criterion. It also means a common identity and culture: for example, religion, language, customs, institutions, and history. Both racial and ethnic groups are positioned by social definitions. Race is determined by physical criteria, while cultural factors would generally determine ethnicity. Race signifies exclusion while ethnicity signifies subculture. Immigration from postcolonial countries to colonizing countries forces postmodern societies to explore the inherent ambiguity that arises from the inability of immigrant groups to assimilate physically with the white dominant societies. This incongruity has devastating implications because it assumes that differences in physical and biological characteristics of humans justify discrimination and hierarchical ranking in society. To minimize this danger, multiculturalism should allow us to live in a democratic non-racist society by raising consciousness, especially in education, about the ignorance and bias involved in the perpetuation of the myth of superior social ranking on the basis of colour (skin pigmentation), and other physical and biological characteristics.

Among strategies used to evade but also selectively invoke racism is the equation of ethnicity with race. Technically, this juxtaposition places white ethnic groups (Europeans) in the same category as racially different groups. Unfortunately, however, the reality is such that the term *ethnic* has evolved to imply non-Western groups, who are thus relegated to a lesser status. Although in the strict sense we are all ethnics, the search for identity produces contradictions that sometimes create us against them (as in Quebec) nationalist-based proclamations with pejorative connotations. Both ethnic and immigrant have come to mean non-white groups and have, therefore, taken on racial connotations. Of course, all immigrants are not non-white, nor are all non-whites immigrants. Yet white immigrants merge quickly with the dominant group while non-white people who have been in the host country for generations are still referred to as immigrants. As such, even when the terms of race and ethnicity are not synonymous, the "criteria of racial differentiation [are] just those for ethnicity" (Goldberg, 1992, p. 555). "What pigmentation often stands for ... is a range of encultured characteristics that include (but need not be limited to) a model of dress, bearing, gait, hairstyle, speech, and so forth" (p. 553). With the rejection of the biological definition of race, the cultural conception of race has slowly assumed currency. This indicates a shift in the strategies of racism from overt to covert forms. Those who experience exclusion from dominant economic, political, and cultural institutions, and face social distance, develop a consciousness of race as a painful encounter. On the other hand, ethnicity does not signify obvious barriers; ethnic minorities are led to believe in social and occupational mobility if they "acquire the credentials of inclusion, principally through education, training, and legal protection against discrimination" (Aronowitz, 1992, p. 53). It is actually because of the reality of these complex and intersecting meanings and programs of race and ethnicity that the two constructs are used interchangeably in this book, because in Western societies they produce similar reactions in social relations.

Constructions of difference have produced several terms for racially distinguishable groups. The official Canadian expression used to refer to non-white groups who originate from the countries of Asia, Africa, and Latin America is "visible minorities" (who are aware that they are invisible in the corridors of power). Visible minorities are defined by skin colour in a society where whiteness is taken to be the norm. The expression "people of colour" is used by these groups to refer to themselves. Here, even if whites, by racing and ethnicizing others, want to present themselves as non-ethnic and, by extension, colourless (Leistyna, 1997; Morrison, 1993), people of colour would emphatically state that whites are not actually so much colourless, for it is exactly those impactful meanings of their colour, and not an unseen, beyond the horizon state of belonging to a primordial norm, that has, at least previously, facilitated the privileges they enjoy. As for the expression "minority group," it refers to categories of people who do not necessarily form a numerical minority vis-à-vis the referent group, but are deprived due to their lack of power. As educational issues go in this regard, Ogbu (1992) previously distinguished between immigrants who are voluntary minorities, and those who are involuntary, or caste-like, minorities, such as Native groups who were internally colonized, or African Americans who were brought in as slaves. Further, Ogbu (1992) pointed to the significance of differentiating between the educational needs of voluntary (immigrant) and non-voluntary (caste-like) minorities. The problems of involuntary minorities are those of secondary cultural differences that develop as a response to contact with the dominant culture. They are often defined in opposition to the dominant culture. Cultural inversion occurs when minorities see certain aspects of a dominant culture to be inappropriate. These in-group behaviour patterns may take the form of different styles of communication (words and phrases), or the rejection of values such as academic achievement being synonymous with acting white. Educators must be sensitive to the psychological pressures of peers to remain in-group.

Generally, voluntary minorities would be characterized by primary cultural differences (such as discipline, freedom, behaviour patterns). Voluntary minorities initially face a variety of problems, but these are primarily due to cultural differences, which existed before the minority and dominant cultures came in contact. Difficulties are related to interpersonal and inter-group relations because minority groups may start school with different cultural assumptions, language problems, and differences in behavioural and cognitive styles. For example, cultural norms may prevent students from class participation. This is particularly so among females. However, because they do not necessarily give up their own cultural beliefs, they tend to adopt a strategy of accommodation. Cultural and language differences are seen as barriers to be overcome in order to achieve their ultimate goals of good education and employment. Voluntary minority students are able to overcome what they see as barriers, and succeed in school eventually.

A further distinction needs to be made within groups of voluntary minorities. Studies have been done on the educational and economic success of some Asian minority groups in Britain, the United States, Australia, and Canada. Voluntary minority groups consist of heterogeneous ethnocultural clusters. Those who succeed academically do so despite their negative experiences of racism and discrimination. Studies indicate that child-rearing and cultural factors such as motivational values account for differences in the academic achievement of the successful minority students. Finally, one could deduce from Ogbu's seminal studies that, at least in one important way, it is the relationship of the voluntary minority group with the dominant culture that entrenches enduring regimes of internalized low self-esteem that limits the overall achievement in the world of involuntary minorities.

Racism

Racism, for all pragmatic considerations, has no biological basis, and is essentially an ideology of power that stratifies people on the basis of biological and cultural characteristics. While the educational milieu in Canada has been previously silent on racism (although anti-racist education has been present in British schools for close to three decades), recent work by George Dei (1996), among others, has shed an important light on the issue, including the de-mythologizing of the relationship between minorities and dominant groups in public spaces of schooling that consistently create enduring favourable conditions for the latter. In this regard, Dei described the practice of anti-racist education as:

> a proactive, process-oriented approach to helping educators and students negotiate and gain insight into the racial and ethnocultural differences they may bring to the classroom. Anti-racism

education has a rich theoretical base, and an everyday practical grounding for educators who wish to both understand and engage issues of racial and ethnocultural difference in their classrooms. It is also about investigating and changing how schools deal with issues of white privilege and power sharing (Dei, 1996, p. 9).

Moreover, the stereotype of immigrants being uneducated is unfounded. In countries such as Canada, Australia, and the United States, some immigrant groups have higher average levels of education compared with native-born groups. In Canada especially, the case of African Canadians is an interesting one. While they have higher educational achievements per capita relative to the Canadian average, African Canadians are also more likely to have lower levels of long-term employment and income, partially due to their racial categorization (Torczyner et al., 1997)

Both in its overt and covert forms, racism in Western societies is now seen as a system of discrimination directed mainly at non-white people, and race, gender, and class-related episodes of discrimination in schools are not uncommon. Racial slurs, jokes, name-calling, and acts of physical and emotional violence (the last being skilfully camouflaged in a number of legally unassailable methodologies) are experienced. In such unwelcoming learning environments, some students might feel singled out as troublemakers if they resist differential treatment. In other instances, these same students will feel ignored in class. And despite all the noise made about multicultural education, critical pedagogy, and student-centered, dialogic modalities of learning, it should be safe to assert that current public spaces of schooling in North America do not effectively deal with these and related difference-deficit issues in any systematic manner (Nieto, 1992; Macedo, 1995).

Race discrimination in economic, political, and cultural situations has strengthened race consciousness among those who experience the multiple pains of exclusion from the dominant society and culture. The United Nations *International Convention on the Elimination of all Forms of Racial Discrimination* defines the term *racial discrimination* to mean "any distinction, exclusion, restriction or preference based on race, colour, descent, or national or ethnic origin which has the purpose or effect of nullifying or impairing the recognition, enjoyment or exercise, on an equal footing, of human rights and fundamental freedoms in the political, economic, social, cultural or any other field of public life" (Article 1). As such, some of what Kovel (1984) identified earlier can still be seen within the current structures of modern racism. That is, there are at least three types of racism: dominative racism, in which the status of race privileges white dominant groups; aversive racism, which involves separation and avoidance; and meta-racism, in which overt forms of racial superiority do not exist, but white domination and policies of exclusion have negative implications for people of colour. These types can be identified with different periods in the history of Western immigrant societies, although both aversive and meta-racism definitely coexist in contemporary times.

Class

Class represents economic and social status, and the factors that determine class are income, education, and occupation. Class can also be measured in terms of work by the apposition of opposites, such as skilled versus unskilled, intellectual versus manual, and professional versus blue collar. The basis of distinction is the occupational level, as well as consumption patterns, such as the make of car in a consumer culture where the majority have cars.

Ethnicity, culture, and race assume significance in relation to class because they can be used to mean socio-economic status (Goldberg, 1992). Class has meaning only within a given context. Previously, for example, when women were mostly at home, they tended to assume the class affiliations of the significant males in their lives: father or husband. The combined effects of ethnicity and gender on class are complex. Class affiliations not only influence educational achievement and the field and level of study, they also determine life chances in terms of jobs, friendships, and partners, as well as networks. Cultural theorists point to the family as the single most important factor in counteracting the egalitarian goals of the school. Not only are realistic educational aspirations related to parents' class, but also to cultural capital, in terms of linguistic skills, confidence, motivation, parental time, and guidance, all of which determine school success.

Poverty, on the other hand, is class-related. Poverty particularly affects specific groups: women, racial minorities, and the elderly. In Western countries, poverty affects a sizeable number of children. For example, it is estimated that one in five Canadian children lives in poverty. While poverty is a comparative term and does not indicate the same intensity in all countries of the world, poor children are most likely to be at risk. Statistics show a clear link between education and poverty: the lower the level of education of the head of the family, the greater the chance that the family will fall into poverty. Lower levels of education are also associated with higher levels of unemployment. In a society where economic achievement is highly valued and constitutes a measure of success, schools construct failures out of those who are not economically privileged.

Classism

Poverty is especially damaging to children whose undernourishment, substandard housing and unfavourable living conditions all combine to create a cycle of underachievement. Absences from school due to sickness are a part of this cycle, all of which results in a sense of hopelessness and alienation on the part of the children, and eventually to dropping out of school. Schools fail working class children through the organizational culture, an irrelevant and alienating curriculum, and by teaching and evaluation processes that give a negative sense of self. Schools fail the children of the poor, and extend the cycle of underachievement. It is the inter-generational aspect of poverty that prevents poor people from taking advantage of education. The profound implications of poverty upon education are seen in the dropout rates that remain invisible in personal experiences of failure and impeded opportunities.

Gender

Gender is defined by feminist theorists as a social construct. *Sex*, by contrast, is determinable by definite physical and biological differences. Societal discrimination that occurs against women is founded on gender distinctions. Considerable prejudice is verbalized by using sexist vocabulary and stereotyping sex roles, hence the term *sexism*. For some time, psychologists have been aware of gender differences in their studies of human behaviour. However, the studies have traditionally dealt mainly with male subjects, and have been interpreted by male researchers. This has led to constructing male behaviour as the norm, and female behaviour as deviating from that norm because they are different.

Studies indicate that differences in gender are at the root of social subordination of females, and are constructed along several spheres. Carol Gilligan (1982) provides insights into these differences, which are useful for educators. The most obvious differences are in values. Boys are more concerned with rules, and girls with relationships. Boys' orientation is positional, in competition or comparison with others, whereas for girls it is personal. Boys focus on individuation, such as separation from parents, and on individual achievement, while girls focus on love and care. Boys and girls differ in their construction of the moral problem. For boys, morality is tied to fairness and competing rights, and involving modes of thinking that are abstract and formal. For girls, morality involves responsibility, and is contextual and narrative. Identity construction is also different. For boys, separation and individuation are critically tied to masculine identity, which is shaped in relation to the world. For girls, femininity is defined through attachment rather than separation from their mothers; it is formed in relationships of intimacy. This does not, however, mean that they have weaker ego boundaries. Generally, it is girls who emerge with a stronger sense of empathy, or understanding of others' needs and feelings. Boys identify with autonomous thinking, logical decision-making, competition, and success. These attributes are associated with masculinity. They are also the attributes that prevail in society and school. When girls do not exhibit these qualities they fail. When they do, they are considered unfeminine. Of the two components of the achievement-motivation construct, the hope for success and the motive to avoid failure are masculine characteristics. Girls, on the other hand, may show anxiety when dealing with competition and, with culture playing an important role, may even show a zoned and specifically located fear of success.

Sexism

Education has mostly been an arena for the preservation of male power and ideology. Sexism in education has been amply substantiated over the last decade in terms of its perpetuation and impact on the life chances of girls. Equality of opportunity can be analyzed in four ways. The first is equal access to the educational system, which depends both on the availability of facilities and disposition to take advantage of these facilities. The second is equal participation in the educational system, which refers to their equal treatment in the curriculum and school culture. The third is equal educational results, and the fourth is equal educational effects on their life chances in terms of availability of jobs and ability to work.

While differences such as race, ethnicity, gender, and class should not make a difference as to how we treat each other, the social construction of each of these categories make them difficult to ignore. Educators must be aware that these differences affect the behaviour of both the person who discriminates and those who are discriminated against. Young (1990) asserts that discursive, or self-conscious, racism and sexism have receded to some degree in societies committed to formal equality. They are at odds with proper behaviour, and politically incorrect (although some individuals, groups and intellectuals may still express them). Subtle and covert forms of discrimination are still widespread.

Prejudice

Prejudice is a pre-judgment. It is an opinion, which is made in advance, and is not based on evidence. It is a negative attitude towards members of a group. Like a stereotype, it is a baseless generalization, but each construct, prejudice and stereotype is independent of the other. For example, one can be prejudiced without having a stereotype and vice versa.

Until recently, it was thought that racial prejudice was absent in young children, and that it only developed with age. Later research findings (Aboud, 1993) show that prejudice is present in children as young as five, and that prejudices in the very young are not necessarily influenced by their parents. Rather, they are related to children's egocentrism, or inability to accept a different perspective, as well as to their inability to differentiate individual from group differences. Prejudice declines by age eight or nine as a function of socio-cognitive development in two areas. Role-taking skills help the child to reconcile racial differences, and perceptual differentiation helps the child to attend to individual rather than racial differences. Programs to reduce prejudice should take these factors into consideration. Prejudicial behaviour in children influences their choice of friends. Those who are ostracized or excluded suffer damaging effects to their social development. What is perhaps most disconcerting is that minority group children develop prejudices towards their own groups, so that both majority (white) and minority (non-white) group children learn to prefer the dominant group in society (Aboud, 1993).

Prejudices sometimes involve stereotypes. Stereotypes are social constructs in which people are identified in terms of fixed images regarding groups, which are always associated with specific attributes, particularly those easily distinguishable by colour or culture (Ghosh, 1996). Derived from its usage in printing, the word stereotype is now generally used to refer to attitudes that imprint a certain picture of reality on others. While it is easy for those who commit the act of stereotyping against those who are perceived different, and in most cases politically and socio-economically weaker, the long-term effects of this behaviour on its victims could be highly problematic, with many negatively based socio-cultural and other implications and possibilities.

Discrimination

Discrimination is the behaviour resulting from prejudice, which grants or denies individuals or groups opportunities and rewards based upon characteristics such ethnicity, sex, class, religion, and language. The central issue, which affects all children—white and non-white—is discrimination based on distinctive characteristics. Discrimination may take several forms. Denial of equality/equity, directly or indirectly on the basis of race and ethnicity, is racism. The same behaviour based on sex is sexism, and it may also be based on socio-economic factors such as class. Discrimination such as racist, sexist, or class intolerant behaviour operates at three levels: personal or individual; cultural (in the larger society and in school); and institutional (in terms of arrangements in society and school such as patterns of school administration). Regardless of people's intentions, cultural and institutional discrimination has damaging and injurious results on society. Discriminatory behaviour is also a result of individual attitudes. At the personal level, discrimination is the denial of respect or rights to individuals, and inferior treatment on the basis of race, ethnicity, gender, and class. In any form, discrimination reflects power difference.

Education and Difference

Schools play a significant role in maintaining—whether directly or indirectly, by omission or commission—the racism, sexism, and classism schemes that are prevalent in society. The results of discrimination affect society in a variety of ways, socially and economically. Poverty, racism, and sexism are related to dropout rates, crime and illiteracy. Racism, sexism, and classism are specific forms of discrimination, as noted above. But there are conceptual parallels among them: stereotyping—of minority ethnocultural groups, women, and working class children; exclusion of their experiences, which keeps them off the record and makes them invisible by giving them reactive, docile roles as objects; domination through universalization of the dominant middle class norm; marginalization because of differences from the way competence is defined in the dominant group's image in school and society.

From a critical pedagogy perspective, while multicultural and intercultural education theoretically give equal access to all ethnocultural groups, these programs have not eliminated discrimination, nor have they resulted in equal participation in the educational or economic spheres. Racism in school results from a spectrum of attitudes, ranging from negative stereotypes and low expectations from teachers, to tracking and labelling (blaming the victim). Student expressions of racism vary from name-calling and cruel jokes to physical attacks and gang violence. Media reports indicate that racial tensions in some multi-ethnic high schools, especially ethnic gang violence, have reached troublesome proportions in certain urban centres. While these influences abound, pedagogically the issue is how the historical and social constructions of whiteness and difference are learned. More critically, what opportunities are given to students to deconstruct these conceptions as implying reality. The pedagogical aim is to focus on how students "learn to identify, challenge, and rewrite such representations" (Giroux, 1993, p. 21).

Educators must have an understanding of what effects the conceptualization of difference will have on students (Bang, 2002; Diamond and Moore, 1995). The educational implication is that stereotypes and prejudices close children's minds, because they reject contradiction and critical thinking based on facts. One of the most important things educators need to keep in mind is that it is the depiction of the categories of race, gender, and class as monolithic entities that lead to stereotypes and prejudices. Unconscious meanings and reactions are still widespread, and "reproduce relations of privilege and oppression. Judgments ... are made unconsciously ... and these judgments often mark, stereotype, devalue, or degrade some groups" (Young, 1990, p. 133). They could then react in various ways, which may not all be associated with discrimination: avoidance, antagonism, stereotyping, discrimination, and being patronizing. For students, painful encounters with educators can result in their being silenced, humiliated, or made to feel invisible and deficient. Unconscious reactions often lead to devaluation of groups, and affect judgments of individual competence. In the end, how an educational milieu deals with difference will be greatly affected by the underlying constructions of identity, which is the focus of our discussion in this next segment.

Constructions of Identity

The common aim of multicultural education programs should be a pluralistic outlook, and the development of a positive self-concept in minority group children. Specifically, this deals with student attitudes, and involves student self-esteem and identity. Positive aspects of these constructs require positive conceptions of one's racial, ethnic, gender, and class affiliations through the school. The question, then, is how can educators facilitate student attempts at making sense of the self and the other in the process of empowerment.

It is important to recognize that immigrants experience culture differently, and their construction of identity becomes a hybrid, being reproduced within a different framework belonging to the dominant society (Bhabha, 1994). For second-generation children, what is recreated in the new environment can never be the same as what was left behind by their parents. The basic traditional principles, however, guide choices, and provide confidence and continuity. This causes conflict in second generation children due to the dissonance between home and school culture as well as values. The process of identity construction, especially in immigrants, may not be enveloped by tranquil cultural parameters, but could be laden with antagonistic encounters, and with at least temporary identity upheavals. As Matustik (1998) noted, the promise of the cultural third space, if it ever materializes, surely would initially disadvantage the cultural representations of the situationally marginalized populations.

For visible minorities, the apparent distinction in colour and/or culture produces a sense of discomfort and forces them to define themselves, to say who they are and what constitutes their identity.

This self-definition produces conflict in identity formation, because traditions are being reconstructed through fragmentation. Ethnic identity changes, and the evolution of this identity is part of the democratic process in postmodern, multicultural societies. As Ogbu (1992) pointed out, for involuntary minorities, school culture is seen as displacing their social identity. They may cope with their subordination by withdrawing, dropping out, or with new forms of culture and behaviour. This is often achieved by developing oppositional social identities and cultural frames of reference in opposition to the dominant culture. The withdrawing as well as oppositional social identities, while they may lessen the pain of subordination, are nevertheless new tools in the hands of the dominant group, who not only exploit the new formation of social identities, but construct the new developments as inherently inferior, therefore confirming their right to dominance and to continued politico-economic power.

Acculturation—the transference of cultural components from dominant to minority groups—causes stress, which is indicative of the internal anxiety felt by those who feel isolated by being separated from the dominant culture and marginalized by not being active participants in their ethnic culture. Assimilation causes the greatest stress by pulling away from ethnic ties. Those who experience integration—who feel at home in both cultural environs—experience the least stress, perhaps even a sense of belonging (Krishnan and Berry, 1992). In these contexts, it is the immigrant groups that face the greatest threat to self-concept, which makes them vulnerable to emotional disorders. Identity crisis is a common problem because ethnic and national identity are treated as conflicting. It is an us-versus-them politics of location, in which visible minority groups remain immigrants in the perception of mainstream groups, even after several generations. This is a philosophy of exclusion in which dominant groups perpetuate an ideology of founding nations by excluding the Native population and others (visible minorities in particular) through white racism. The onus is on dominant groups to be inclusive because minority groups do not define the parameters of separation.

Politics of Identity

The politics of identity have significant implications for educational success. The dynamics of identity and identification in modern society are complex. Identity politics is a response to unequal relations resulting from differences between social groups. Over the last three decades, new identities have emerged. It is only recently that other categories such as race, ethnicity, and gender have been added to class in studies of group identity. Feminism has brought other subject positions into the political and social agenda. In feminist poststructuralist discourse, the struggle over identity within the subject is inseparable from the struggle over the meaning of identities and subject positions in the larger society. The contradictions of gender, class, and race produce a low self-concept, which is accompanied by a sense of alienation and vulnerability.

Ethnic identity, on the other hand, is not an entity. Rather, its construction is a complex process in which a variety of factors have their impact. Some of these factors are strongly informed by gender, but the impact of gender in the representation of ethnic identity is rarely examined in research, thus making women's experiences and gender-related aspects of ethnicity invisible (Phinney, 1990). If there is some evidence that ethnic identity declines with generations, it is also known that ethnicity remains, in almost all parts of the world, a political process of positioning within the boundaries of a collectivity, based on notions of common origin and interest. In addition, constructions of ethnicity and ethnic identity are fluid and changing, according to the context of people's lives. Moreover, they are not homogenous categories, and operate across gender and class. An interesting phenomenon is the globalization of identity politics based on international economic position and interest, which defies national boundaries and traditional class affiliations. The shifts in identity are organized around global survival. This brings issues of environment and sustainable development to the forefront, making social justice and liberation issues critical.

Implications for Multicultural Education

The daily experiences that shape the identity of minority group students, the psycho-social impact of prejudice, and discrimination based on race, ethnicity, gender, and class, are of great significance, more so with the increasing ethnic and racial makeup of schools and society. Key questions relate to the implications of identity for self-esteem and school achievement, and of ethnic identity for integration with and relationship to the dominant culture.

The aim of multicultural education is to help all children develop identities that will give them a positive self-concept, and make them critical and transformative citizens in democratic, multicultural societies (Davidman and Davidman, 2000). As Cornbleth and Waugh (1995, p. 37) observed, "a multiple-perspectives approach would include the experiences and points of view of various participants throughout the events being studied ... participants' voices would be heard as directly as possible." The success of multicultural education programs will depend upon their ability to create unity within the diversity—to integrate ethnic identity at the individual level with a national identification.

The initial trend in multicultural education in Western societies has been to focus on ethnic diversity and heritage, and teach about immigrant cultures, rather than to focus on self-concept (personal identity) and ethnic (social) identity, and how those two merge with an overall national (political) identity. The result, then, is that ethnic cultural islands float around without being anchored. The individual student's attempt is to make sense of the self and the other, or of the personal, social, and political modes. This is a subjective experience, which explains the variety in experiences, and underscores the dynamic, often contradictory and conflicting, dimensions of interactions and personal identity. Identities are not fixed or rigid categories. Rather, to quote Stuart Hall, identity "is a matter of 'becoming' as well as of 'being' ... [a construct that is] subject to the continuous 'play' of history, culture and power" (Hall, 1990, p. 225). As such, children of differing ethnocultural descent in classrooms are not what their parents are or were because of their positional identities in history and culture. Their experiences and identities are constructed in relation to their gender, class, and race, as well as their ethnicity (which is mediated by culture) and their location in history.

The question, then, is how educators can facilitate students' desires to make sense of the self and the other in the process of positive self-concept and empowerment. Since the problems in school are caused by differences in cultural content and practices, as a first step, teachers can help tremendously by learning about the students' cultural backgrounds and by understanding their processes of identity formation and deformation. This does not imply knowledge of multiple cultures and traditions. Rather, it involves a broad understanding of, and empathy towards, diverse cultures, as well as an interest in each student. Teachers can organize classrooms and programs in a manner that encourages interaction and communication among students, and involve parents in the education of their children. The teacher's role is to help students interpret their social relations, rather than treat individual students' cultures as artifacts. The strategy is to separate the two aspects of ethnicity: identity and culture. It is of crucial importance in multicultural education to focus on identity development: gender and ethnicity at the individual level, and social and political at the community and national levels.

The differences in the cultural content of minority culture children, resulting in differences in communication and interaction styles, cognitive and learning styles, make it necessary for the teacher, as mediator in the education process, to develop a knowledge base on which to build understanding. Knowledge of students is imperative if teachers are to guide their learning experiences and lead students to see the connections between what is learned in school and their lived experiences. Education is not merely collecting disjointed knowledge; rather, it is acquiring conceptual schemes. Learning is to connect and to make meaning, and must be built on students' experiences and what they know. It behooves us as educators to understand student experiences, and how identities are produced differently. Only then can teachers provide students with the analytical tools to deal with problems of unresolved identities, and challenge experiences of racism, sexism, and other inequities. Erikson (1963), who began identity research, considered educational practices as largely determining identity traits or loss of identity. While emphasizing early childhood experiences, he drew attention to the possibility of changing identities because identity cannot be separated from the construction of the world around us. The idea of self is culture-specific, but influenced by the realm of social experiences (including curriculum and role models), perceptions, and acceptance by others, both in school and society.

In a review of both qualitative and quantitative research from diverse fields on ethnic identity, Phinney (1990) identified three approaches that explained ethnic identity formation. All of them viewed ethnic identity as dynamic and changing over time, as well as varying with the situation. The first approach is that social identity theory explained self-concept as related to how the dominant group views a particular group. The studies indicate that positive self-concept may be related to positive ethnic identification in high status groups. Conversely, lower status ethnic group membership is related to poorer self-concept. The second approach is that there are two themes in the acculturation framework: a linear model, which assumes that the stronger the ethnic identity the weaker the identification with the majority society; and a two-dimensional model, which asserts that the two identities (ethnic and dominant culture) are separate and independent. It is possible to have a strong identification both with one's own ethnic culture as well as with the dominant culture, indicating integration, while weak identification with both is indicative of marginality. The third approach examines identity formation at the individual level in a developmental way, as a complex process by which people construct their ethnicity. Phinney proposed a three-stage progression in identity construction, from unexamined ethnic identity, to a period of exploration, and finally, to achieved ethnic identity. The first and second processes are especially crucial for schools. The first period may be characterized by a lack of interest in one's ethnicity. In the case of minority ethnic group students, this could lead to a preference for the dominant culture, or a view of ethnicity based on the opinion of others. The second phase involves development of a personal understanding of ethnicity. Teachers should be sensitive to these phases.

Empowerment

The concepts of empowerment and empowering are radical and political. The root word in both empowerment (a sense of control) and empowering (fostering, or enabling a sense of power) is power. The prefix em- indicates bringing into a condition, while the suffixes -ment and -ing imply ongoing action and process. The basic understanding of power is ability; it is also capability and strength in action. Empowerment, then, is bringing into a state of ability or capability to act (Ghosh, 1996). Sociological definitions of power tend to be relational, and power is usually seen as a means to have control over something or someone. It is also seen in terms of a commodity that people either have or do not have (Sleeter, 1991). The emergence of postmodern theory has led to an interpretation of power as power by consensus; that is, power *with*, rather than power *by* force, or power *over* people. Paulo Freire (2000) has emphasized that people are never powerless. Even oppressed people display power by acts of resistance. His philosophy of education is based on empowerment. This means power *with* people in a cooperative sense, not power *over* people. As bell hooks (2000) points out, it is the power of oppressed people (women) that we must focus on if they are to move from the margin to the centre. To empower students, therefore, it is not enough to simply tell them that they are empowered, or to superficially praise their so-called cultural package (which generally connotes the existence of a problem that needs justification). To effectively empower students from all backgrounds in today's multicultural settings, Diamond and Moore (1995) want us to affirm and acknowledge students' cultural backgrounds, help them to develop positive self-images, and facilitate their ability to construct their own meaning from what they read and write. Educators (must) realize that there will have to be radical changes in what and how children are taught and what they learn if we are to educate all children. As teachers take on new roles and adopt and refine their practices, they need to consider the factors and contexts that necessitate these modifications; they need to consider the new realities of society and the classroom.

Conversely, students are disabled by school experiences that do not develop academic and emotional foundations. It is important to understand that student empowerment is both a means to academic performance and an educational end. Empowering education implies creating conditions that allow for the transformation of students' potential power to activity or empowerment. It suggests learning as a process of inquiry and discovery, where knowledge is regarded as something that can be personally acquired, not given as a fixed entity. It perceives the curriculum as one that gives full expression to multiple voices, and to development as personal growth, with schools operating as communities. Empowerment means that students can articulate and defend values, and also demonstrate them. It involves a pivotal role for the teacher in facilitating and creating an interdependent relationship with students. Students who are empowered will acquire the necessary educational tools to combine the conceptual foundations of their world with practical possibilities in order to change their lives. Multicultural education places power with the teacher and the students in the classroom, where everyone develops the power to learn, and the power to imagine.

Dealing with Difference

On one hand, identity and empowerment are influenced by the recognition of others, to the extent that misrecognition, or not giving due recognition, constitutes a form of oppression (Taylor, 1994) and is disempowering. On the other hand, the concepts of identity and empowerment are closely related to the notion of difference and the politics of difference. Education plays a significant role in the way people recognize, identify, and construct differences in others. Dealing with the politics of recognition and difference involves the cognitive, affective, and moral spheres. Teachers will undoubtedly have instinctive feelings that may involve an ethic of caring. However, there are many practical ways in which educators could deal with difference, keeping in mind that the educational goal is not the creation of meaning around difference, but the affirmation of difference.

1. Incorporating Difference

The way in which schools play a major part in reproducing differences has been explained in detail through the theories of social and cultural reproduction we saw in chapter one. Generally, schools validate (or invalidate) student experiences and identities, with race, gender, and class representations constructed largely through the school culture and curriculum. The understanding that knowledge is socially constructed offers opportunities for teachers to make learning relevant to all students, and involve students in creating their own knowledge irrespective of gender, class, or ethnic background. This understanding can lead to reflections on how social phenomena become defined and organized: what the world looks like through other's eyes, and how students think about themselves through a different voice. Questions about the organization of knowledge will include all those who do not fit the male dominant culture model that has represented the norm for so long.

Issues of difference should be explicit topics for discussion, in order to develop greater awareness of otherness through sharing experiences. The psychosocial consequences of the culture conflicts faced by ethnic and visible minority children and adolescents, or of being female and working class, are related to how race, ethnicity, gender, and class are constructed as difference. Teachers must deal with this, and examine the politics of difference. Educators can find guidelines in poststructuralist theory that challenge the idea of fixed identities through deconstructing master narratives. A necessary part of this project, however, would be questions on the concept of whiteness and the advantages that it entails. Dominant groups need to be taught to challenge oppression, especially because their privileged position tends to make it difficult for them to see the world critically.

2. Discussing Difference and Discrimination

Good education, which is always a culturally sensitive education, implies honest communication. It is necessary to uncover how

Eurocentric discourses of identity suppress difference, heterogeneity, and multiplicity in efforts to maintain hegemonic relations of power (Giroux, 1991). It is important that teachers, along with the students, examine new ways to understand how power works in constructing race, class, and gender, and how power differentials are maintained through racism, sexism, and classism. In particular, when students are from marginalized segments of society, this will involve the deliberate and courageous crossing of boundaries by teachers who must mediate multiple identities, abilities, and expectations so all students could achieve their potential (Bang, 2002). Even if they want to, educators in today's pluralistic societies cannot escape from their responsibility to discuss racism, sexism, stereotypes, prejudice, and discrimination, all of which play an important role in constructing the we-and-they relations.

In these important instances of students' lives, the focus must be on cultural difference and how to deal with it, rather than on cultural diversity and similarity in groups, which depoliticizes multiculturalism. It is equally important for students to learn what inequality means to people, both in school and in society: the harm it does to students, the pain it inflicts, and the injustice it embodies. White racism, patriarchy, and class domination must be examined so that domination does not go unchecked. It is essential to understand that racism is produced by whites through the enforcement of skin colour as a category of difference leading to social hierarchy, and imposed by whites on non-whites (Scheurich, 1993). In society, all people are racialized, gendered, and classed, and each person is subjected daily to the complex effects of membership in each of these groups in significant ways (Scheurich, 1993). Students must understand why eradicating racism requires changing the behaviour of white people, just as eliminating sexism involves changing male behaviour, although the empowerment of the victims is the other side of the coin.

Textbooks, teacher interaction, organizational structure, and social experiences in school provide the framework for the construction of race as white or black by telling students their status in society and their location in the power structure. If the scientific basis of evolution is being reinterpreted based on new DNA evidence, why are racist, sexist, and class-biased texts not eligible for deconstruction and scrutiny? If fossils can be re-dated with new evidence, surely racism and sexism can be challenged in relation to social evolution in human rights, justice, and equality.

Ignoring controversial issues and differences, and focusing on similarities, as many multicultural education programs do, is harmful for both dominant and minority group students. Via the quasi-proverbial crimes of commission and omission, educators are absolving everyone, which can only assure the continuities of the conventional regimes of marginalization that have created the status quo in the first place. As Darling-Hammond (2002) notes, the belief among many educators, who theoretically welcome the core principles of multicultural education, that focusing on difference will create separatism is, on all accounts, wrong. Those who take this position, writes Darling-Hammond,

> fail to understand that finding out what we have in common requires that we begin communicating from the vantage points of our separate experiences. Each of us [students and teachers] has to find a way to express and locate our own experiences within that conversation in order to be validated as learners and human beings. This allows us then to connect with new knowledge and with the experiences of others. Far from encouraging separatism, acknowledgement of diverse experiences helps create new associations that help us ultimately to build the common ground on which a more inclusive and powerful learning community can rest (2002, p. 3).

In the event that this mutually enriching understanding among learners is not ascertained and encouraged, the long-term effects of the schooling experience can have oppressive consequences. Students who are different from the privileged norm in their cultural experiences, racial qualities, and gender may not understand their disadvantage in relation to the established standard. This can result in perpetuating their barriers and maintaining the status quo. Moreover, the established norm is made to look objective and unbiased. In addition, these standards are internalized as universal, and any variation is seen as failure.

Teaching methods must include the analysis and deconstruction of racist and sexist materials and social interactions, because the manner in which individuals deal with these conflicts influences identity formation. In addition, teachers must deal immediately with overt racism such as name-calling, and physical or emotional violence. Equally important, they must be trained to identify and address systemic factors that may unintentionally result in discriminatory impact. Teachers can start with all students, by promoting equality in the school culture, integrating anti-racist and anti-sexist education, and by making the environment culturally diverse. The *raison d'être* of multicultural education is to enable students to redefine reality by breaking out of stereotypical roles, expectations, and labels, thus reconstructing their new, emergent situations.

3. Racial/Ethnic and Cultural Identity

In education, what we reveal to a student about himself or herself as an ethical and intellectual being has the power to, at least selectively, shape his or her academic confidence, inter-personal relations, and even self-efficacy, to effectively deal with life's diverse and continually differentiated challenges. Greatly attached to these possibilities are the psychosocial aspects of being a minority, which is determined by the constructions of race, ethnicity, and related identities. If lack of interest in one's ethnicity is phase one, it is crucial that this be reversed in school, in order to avoid being defined by others or becoming marginal individuals. The second phase, the development of personal under-standing, must be facilitated in school experiences through identifica-tion with the curriculum and positive feelings towards one's group. The relationship of racial and ethnic minority groups to their own group is crucial to the self-concept and psychological functioning of individu-als (Phinney, 1990). Immigrant groups face a great threat to self-concept, which makes them vulnerable to emotional disorders. Involuntary minorities develop oppositional identities because they fear the loss of their cultural identities through schooling. Given the educational history of assimilation of Native populations in Australia, the United States, and Canada, it is particularly important to focus on the culture and language of involuntary minorities to serve as bound-ary maintaining markers of their collective identity.

Teachers must be cognizant of oppositional identities, in relation to dominant identity, which can negatively affect school performance. Closely tied to boundary maintenance behaviours and attitudes, oppositional identities are influenced by peer-determined criteria that disapprove of behaviours seen to be at a variance with group identity, such as academic achievement. Girls who show independence and analytical skills face a crisis with their identity as females. For students of other cultures, the aspiration to be academically successful is often in conflict with ethnic identity through oppositional images and messages in the school curriculum and culture. The school must recognize this struggle between group identity and school achieve-ment, and minimize the perception of competing pressures through organizational structures and classroom practices. Students must be helped to develop constructive patterns of thinking and feeling to gain confidence, for this is a key aspect of self-image. Teaching strategies could include cognitive restructuring, modelling, problem solving, and replacing feelings of hopelessness by feelings of adequacy.

What is perhaps most difficult to cope with is that, while second or third generation non-white youth speak with British, Australian, American, or Canadian accents, unlike their parents, they may still experience prejudice and discrimination. "Why am I called an immigrant when I was born here?" is a question many of them ask. Some are confused about their identity. They think of themselves as British, Australian, American, or Canadian, but others' perception of who they are, and their experience of discrimination based on the social construction of ethnicity, race, and gender by these others, can threaten a positive self-concept. The possibility of an identity crisis leading to double alienation—alienation from the primordial group and also from the new significant others—is not entirely remote. And the consequences, educational and eventually economic, that could result from these experiences are not encouraging. Schools play a crucial role in equipping students with the skills with which to sort out the dialectics of identity construction.

If self-concept is related to group status, the development of positive attitudes in dominant and minority group students in class towards other ethnocultural groups is important, in order to avoid status hierarchy. Educators must focus on positive feelings towards all groups in dominant and minority students. Key strategies for educators involve positive ethnic identification in students to promote self-esteem. The assumption is that a child who feels negatively towards his or her ethnic group is unlikely to feel good about themselves. Racial/ethnic identity involves psychological association with one's group. Most research in this area has been done in the field of psychology. Sociological research in this area deals with the social response to the relevant psychological constructs, such as identity and self-concept. Racial or ethnic group membership does not suggest how one identifies oneself. Racial identity is a set of attitudes and behaviours towards one's membership in a group as well as towards the dominant group. Racial identity is also affected by dominant group identification of a person as a member of a particular group.

The paradox is that while one may or may not identify with one's ethnic group, the dominant group is likely to identify a person with a particular racial or ethnic group.

The four most significant components of ethnic identity for education, as Phinney (1990) pointed out, which appear to be the key aspects common across groups, involve the following: self-identification, or how one sees oneself rather than focus on one's descent; a sense of belonging, related to the experience of exclusion or detachment from one's own or the dominant group; positive and negative attitudes toward one's ethnic group leading to pride and pleasure, or denial of ethnic identity and feelings of inferiority; and sensitivity to specific cultural practices such as music, dress, traditional roles, knowledge of history and culture, which may be necessary for understanding individual groups and their experiences. The teacher is not expected to learn all cultures. The need is to enable a positive sense of self through a general knowledge of other cultures, and an empathy with all minority cultures.

Of the two aspects of ethnic identity, external and internal, the school is not very involved with the former. The external aspect includes cultural behaviour patterns such as language and tradition, ethnic networks including family and friends, ethnic institutions such as church, community schools, and media, and ethnic associations including clubs and functions. The internal aspect, which involves images, ideas, and attitudes—such as feelings of obligation and duty, and subjective awareness of belonging—must be reinforced in school. Subjective identity is possible without knowledge of language, and teachers must encourage students to feel good about the internal features of ethnicity.

In a postmodern world, education systems must deal simultaneously with individual ethnic cultures and the construction of identity within a nation as part of world civilization. This is the seeming contradiction between delocalization and relocation of cultural and national identities. The school will play a better role in reinforcing social cohesion at the national level if it is founded on strong individual identities.

4. National Identity

Educational strategies must stress aspects of unity and identification with the country. But they must also generate, in dominant group children, an identity that does not see nationalism in a narrow sense. To be Australian, British, American, or Canadian is not to be only British or French; to be a Quebecois is not to be only of French extraction. The idea is to change the we-and-they configuration, and construct with an inclusive us. This could be done through school and classroom organizations, the curriculum, teacher-student, and student-student relations, and home-school relations. Educators must extend critical pedagogy to look beyond minority groups to mobilize all students, in an effort to promote democratic values and critical thought about what is taken for granted, as well as in reconstituting identities.

Literature, music, science, math, and social studies offer opportunities for deconstruction and locating the other voice. Students can challenge the notions of universal subject and the male, middle class Euro-Canadian cultural standard. Recognizing absences and silences as signifying relations of domination, they can be encouraged to research people left out of history books, such as women from the dominant culture, as well as women and men of other cultures. Math and science classes offer limitless opportunities to relate issues to students' daily lives, and to investigate the history and development of the fields, as well as to explore non-western (and working class) ways of doing things, which may relate to their backgrounds.

All students must be helped to define their location in the class as well as in society, and to explore the possibilities and barriers inherent in that subject position. The teacher must give voice to those students who for cultural or other reasons do not feel part of the class community, through questions and other forms of involvement in group activities. Again, the right and power to speak out may be determined by the width of the space of comfort with which oppressed groups could exercise an authentic sense of identity and the concomitant self-respect and self-development. This is central to their own identity as subjects, rather than being objects in the educational process. If teachers recognize the capacity of children to forge personal meaning, the dynamic, often contradictory and even conflicting dimensions of their experiences as well as their identities will allow for a kaleidoscopic mosaic of meaning.

Schools give mixed messages, because stated policies may show objective standards, whereas individual experiences may be those of discrimination. Role-playing and debates often help in bringing out the affective impact as well as the cognitive meanings of racism, sexism, and classism. Cooperative learning methods give confidence through mutual help. When students cannot relate and are not included, their alienation results in low self-esteem.

5. Syncretic Multicultural Identity

The most challenging issue is the interpretation of conflicts, which becomes apparent in the reconstruction of basic perceptions of group affiliation. This redefinition is searching for a third space, making attempts at syncretism and blending traditions, experimenting with and through identities. An essential project in multicultural education is the development of the national and global dimensions of identity. National identity is a complex issue. The process of integration changes ethnic consciousness. Many historical layers coexist in the mind (Sárkány, 1992), and students cross linguistic, cultural, and social borders continuously. There is a need for the emergence of a new kind of citizenship, which would enable the expression of the multiple identities that we possess. A political system requires a certain degree of social integration to reach a level of understanding. One aspect of this social integration is political integration via citizenship. Schools must recreate a sense of citizenship. In heterogeneous societies it is urgent to develop a unifying political culture in order to prevent disintegration, and this unifying political culture, multiculturalism, must engage all citizens if it is to be more than an ideological claim. Again, educating for effective and productive citizenship will contain important items of teaching for difference that, on all accounts, will be incomplete if it does not educate both the marginalized and the privileged of their respective positions (Sleeter, 1991), complemented by a pragmatic discussion on the possibilities of enfranchising all citizens.

Political culture must, however, remain decoupled from various ethnic cultures (Habermas, 1992). Furthermore, political culture and citizenship in postmodern democracies involve the interconnection between the national and the global, such as the citizens of any one country and citizens of the world in a transnational interdependency. This implies tensions between the centre and the periphery, the political and the social, cultural identity and national loyalty. For education, the significant nexus is between the global, national, and local, or ethnocultural, identities. The challenge for Western immigrant societies, and the task for education, is to deal with the dialectical process of identity construction. The goal is to arrive at a synthesis in order for a syncretic national identity to emerge, and at the same time accommodate the assertions of various cultural, ethnic, and social identities in a postnationalist cultural space (McLaren, 1994).

CONCLUSION

Bhabha (1994) sees the problem of difference as one of the inventions of modernity that has so far distinguished itself in its inability to resolve cultural conflicts. Rather, modernity tends to marginalize, destroy, and obliterate a large variety of world views, both in experiences and through ideas. All forms of identity, including dominant group definitions, are constructed through a dialectical process. Since our self-image and worldviews influence our aspirations and have connotations for what is possible, a focus on identity formation is crucial to the process of education. Quality multicultural education must include the lessons of pluralism. To pretend that differences do not exist is to do disservice to all children, because the other will be disadvantaged while the dominant group will be incapable of coping with the real world, in which the majority are non-Europeans.

Education must enable the increase of one's internal resources, the right to determine one's life choices, and the right to influence social change. In effect, that becomes the essence of empowerment. Finally, if we want to give our students basic human values, and teach them how to be human, as educators we cannot simply be satisfied with understanding our world. We must strive, as much as possible, to change it, so that students of both majority and minority cultures can deal with their differences confidently, knowing that these differences are not relevant to what they could become.

3 | MULTICULTURAL POLICY AND MULTICULTURAL EDUCATION: A CANADIAN CASE STUDY

Legislation cannot change the heart, but it can restrain the heartless.

—*Martin Luther King, Jr.*

C anada was the first country in the world to have a policy of multiculturalism at the federal level. Multiculturalism in Canada is inextricably linked to immigration, and represents a spectacular shift in Canadian social policy, which paralleled the striking alteration to immigration policy. Numerous cultures have coexisted in Canada for hundreds of years. The first dwellers were the Aboriginals, who belonged to different tribes and nations. The English and the French were the first Europeans to arrive in Canada, thousands of years later, establishing their early settlements in Quebec and Ontario. Subsequently, immigrants from other parts of Europe came, and made their homes across other areas of the land. More recently, groups of immigrants from Asian, African, and Latin American countries have settled across the country. The significant point here, and especially important for the analysis undertaken in this work, is the dramatic shift that has taken place in Canadian immigration policy. Initially, it was a policy for the exclusion of non-white groups, including Asians, but also people of colour from south of the border. Later, a major thawing took place towards the same groups, as a result of Asian countries becoming the major source of emigration to contemporary Canada.

Despite the heterogeneous nature of Canadian society, the central fact of Canadian history has been the relations between the English and French charter groups, the aboriginals, and other ethnic groups (Elliott and Fleras, 1990). But these four broad groups have not had equal status, and the English-French equation has dominated Canadian history. The result has been a neglect of the special needs of Aboriginals and other ethnic groups. This chapter will examine the official policy rhetoric aimed at altering this ethnic hierarchy, and the role of education in that political process. Aside from the special situation of the original groups, the First Nations peoples who are moving towards self-government, Canada was historically seen as having two distinct societies. Migration has been a significant factor in the duality of Canadian society, because the new immigrants who opened up the prairie and western provinces assimilated into the English culture. The opening up of the west, which took place in the last decades of the nineteenth century, was not attractive to French Canadians. The textile industry was more attractive for jobs, even though these jobs were located in the United States. It was cheaper and more secure job-wise to go south than to go across the country and westwards. It was also cheaper for pioneers from Europe to go to the prairie provinces than for French Canadians to go west on the train. This fatal hemorrhage, as it has been referred to, resulted in one third of French Canadians going to the United States, according to census data. This migration, along with the defeat of the Métis in Manitoba in 1885, ensured English domination in the west, and the assimilation of Europeans into anglophone culture, especially after World War I, when German and Ukrainian settlers were no longer permitted to teach their languages.

From the point of view of cultural and linguistic policy, English-speaking, or anglophone, Canada comprises nine provinces, and Quebec represents French-speaking, or francophone, Canada. Although Quebec is one of ten provinces, its position in Canada is unique. The province did not sign the 1982 Constitution, and the issue still remains unresolved. Unlike the rest of Canada, which is dominated by people of British origin, Quebec is largely composed of people of French descent, and is linguistically and culturally francophone. Education in Quebec is based on a different philosophy, made possible by the Canadian Constitution, which gives the provinces exclusive authority over education. The federal government's influence in that area is only indirect. Quebec is the only province to have rejected the federal Policy of Multiculturalism (for reasons given below), and to have adopted a policy of Intercultural Education. It is also the only French-speaking province in the country. Most of the provinces have substantial and disparate ethnic minorities, which have integrated to different degrees into the dominant community. The terms ethnic groups (in English-speaking Canada) and cultural communities (in French-speaking Quebec) are used here for describing ethnocultural minority groups because Canadian society has defined them as such for social policy.

The people of the First Nations do not consider themselves as belonging to ethnic groups or cultural communities, because they are the original inhabitants of Canada. It is a paradox that both the terms ethnic groups and cultural communities, when applied exclusively to the other, push these groups to the periphery and give them pejorative connotations. At the same time, by referring to the other, they imply that the dominant groups at the centre are devoid of ethnicity and culture of their own. The terms do not include in their definitions the English and French majorities, or these groups where they are minorities, or First Nations people. However, if multicultural education means the integration of ethnic groups other than the

Aboriginals, the English, and the French, then these aforementioned groups seem to be absolved of any active responsibility in this process of integration. If interculturalism is the integration of cultural communities, will the English, the French, and the First Nations not have to integrate? Having their own school systems, they are outside the education language laws. Who is to be integrated into the larger Canadian society or Quebec society? Briefly, the answer seems to be all those other than the *souche française* (original French), *souche britannique* (original British), and the *autochtone* (Natives).

Immigration History

Immigration policy may represent the perspective as well as the spirit of a given nation and, as such, it changes over time. It is a mechanism used by the current occupants of a territory to screen and determine its partners in the building of a nation (Walker, 1992). The history of Canadian immigration reflects the country's changing vision and represents its national identity. The striking point about early immigration policy in Canada is its exclusionary character, grounded on prevailing conceptions of race. Immigration was based on racial factors, and this dominated Canadian immigration history until 1967, at which time the policy became technically non-racial. Prime Minister Robert Borden illustrates public opinion in 1914:

> ... the immigration of Oriental aliens and their rapid multiplication is becoming a serious menace to living conditions on the West coast and to the future of this country in general. This government shall take immediate action to bring to an end such immigration for residence purposes (Walker, 1992, p. 1).

Walker (1992) identifies four chronological phases in Canadian immigration history, which parallel historical periods as well as public attitudes. The first phase, from Confederation to the first decade of the twentieth century, is identified as the Imperial Outpost, because Canada was a British dominion and seen as an offshoot of Britain. The first Immigration Act was passed in 1896, and it was assumed that most people would come from Britain because the intention was to keep the country British. Towards the end of this period, the need for farmers in the west led to admitting people from northwestern Europe if they were perceived as being assimilable into the English Canadian social structures. In 1907, 20 percent of the immigrants were from central and southern Europe. It was the age of scientific racism, and human beings were categorized genetically as having certain characteristics and abilities. Immigration was based on genetic suitability: admissible races were those who were judged to be suited to the climate and culturally close to Britain (although Canadians were allowed to own slaves, in Quebec, for example). In 1815, even before Confederation, Nova Scotia had passed a resolution prohibiting fugitive American slaves, because "the proportion of Africans already in this country is productive of many inconveniences" (Walker, 1992, p. 3). Yet runaway slaves, led by Harriet Tubman, managed, via the Underground Railroad, to settle in Ontario, as did freed slaves who came to parts of the west, such as Amber Valley in southern Alberta. The policy to exclude, and, if they were already in the country, to isolate certain groups of people was directed against various groups. In the 1840s, blacks were isolated in areas such as Africville in Nova Scotia (Clairmont and Magill, 1999). Later, the Chinese were disenfranchised in British Columbia in 1872, and the Japanese in 1895. This prevented them from voting, and effectively barred them from several other rights including holding public office and obtaining licenses. In 1885, a head tax of $50 was levied as a financial deterrent to Chinese immigrants, and this was increased to $500 in 1903. An agreement with Japan in 1908 voluntarily restricted Japanese immigrants, who were mostly in fishing, boat building, lumbering, and mining.

Another problem for Canadian immigration policy-makers came with immigrants from the subcontinent of India. As British subjects, they could not be openly restricted on racial grounds. So instead, immigrants from India were subjected to a "continuous journey" clause, which meant no stop between points of embarkation and destination, along with a requirement of $200. This virtually eliminated Indian immigration, because there was no direct travel connection between India and Canada that did not involve stops, due to the great distance involved. Meanwhile, by 1907 the first immigrants from India who were already here were disenfranchised in British Columbia. Along with the Chinese and Japanese, they were subjected to social and economic restrictions. All three groups were part of the Vancouver race riots of 1907. The Immigration Act of 1910 overtly used racial criteria for the first time for admission to Canada because, as Mackenzie King said in the Canadian Parliament in 1908, "that Canada should remain a white man's country is believed to be not only desirable for economic and social reasons, but highly necessary on political and national grounds" (Walker, 1992, p. 7).

The second phase, White Dominion, is the period from the second decade of this century to the end of World War II. The shift in the need for unskilled labour resulted in an upsurge of central and southern Europeans, so that by 1913 they composed 48 percent of total immigrants. They were deemed to be culturally inferior to the British and northern European settlers, and a series of measures were enforced to limit immigrants to those from preferred countries. During World War I, eight thousand Ukrainians were interned as enemy aliens. Also at this time, British subjects were defined as natives of white dominions in the British Empire. In 1914, four hundred British subjects from India aboard the Japanese freighter *Komagatu Maru* were denied entry at Vancouver and forced to return.

Immigration from Asian countries became very restricted, and those who were already here were not allowed to bring their families. Parliament was seen as "safeguarding the people of Canada from an influx which it is no chimera to conjure up might annihilate the nation ..." (Walker, 1992, p. 9). The Chinese head tax was not considered effective, and the Chinese Immigration Act was passed in 1923 to exclude their immigration, while the Japanese agreement became more restrictive. At the end of World War I, the British government urged the white dominions to be more generous to immigrants from India. In 1923, five years after the discussion at the Peace Conference, men who had already come to Canada from British India were allowed to apply for entry of their families. At the time of the Depression, immigration was not encouraged, even from western Europe, from which only farmers and female domestic workers were allowed entry. In 1930, Asian immigration was prohibited for the next two decades. With the outbreak of World War II, several hundred German and Italian Canadians and thousands of Japanese Canadians were interned. In reminiscing about this traumatic experience, the Japanese Canadian poet Joy Kagawa says, with the clear gravity of identity and racial undertones:

> What do I remember of the evacuation? / I remember my father telling Tim and me / About the mountains and the train / And the excitement of going on a trip [....] / And I remember how careful my parents were / Not to bruise me with bitterness [....] / And I prayed to the God who loves / All the children in his sight / That I might be white (Kagawa, 1993, pp. 198–99).

Japanese Canadian citizens were also repatriated to Japan, and the federal government repealed its deportation orders in 1947. In 1939, nine hundred Jewish refugees aboard the *St. Louis* were refused entry at Halifax and forced to return to Europe.

The third phase saw a shift in the nation's mood. This took place in the post-World War II years, during which Canada played the part of a Middle Power. The low birth rate during the Depression, industrial growth, and economic expansion after the war, and a general shortage of workers, prompted Prime Minister Mackenzie King to encourage immigration. In the most desirable category were British subjects from Britain and white dominions; the next were American citizens; the third category consisted of wives and children (under 18) of men resident in Canada; and finally, people who would farm in Canada.

World War II provoked debate on a racist immigration policy in a country that had fought against Nazi racism: "Let us have done with superior races and preferred nations," declared E.B. McKay in parliament in 1947 (Walker, 1992, p. 11). The Canadian Citizenship Act in 1946 steered Canada towards a path independent from Britain. The end of the war resulted in large migrations of displaced persons from Eastern Europe. For Canada, they were non-traditional immigrants. It was during that time that France was named a preferred country from which immigrants could come. In 1947, the Chinese Immigration Act was repealed. While this was significant symbolically, Chinese immigration was still restricted, as was the case for other Asians. In 1947, the British Columbia government granted the franchise to residents who were of Chinese and South Asian origin, and in 1949 removed all restrictions from Japanese residents. Despite government attempts to maintain the fundamental composition of Canadian society, the Canadian Labour Congress and other groups pressed for an immigration policy free from racial discrimination.

In addition, the United Nations Universal Declaration on Human Rights (drafted by a Canadian, John Humphrey, who was also the first director of the UN Human Rights Department) and membership in a multiracial Commonwealth made it increasingly difficult for

Canada to maintain a white supremacy policy. In 1950, Germans were allowed entry, due to a liberalization of immigration restrictions aimed at Europeans. The Japanese, however, remained inadmissible as enemy aliens for another two years, and other Asians were still restricted. It was only after Commonwealth unity was threatened that Canada made a symbolic gesture in 1951 to set an annual quota allowing 150 independent immigrants from India (this was doubled in 1957), 100 from Pakistan, and 50 from Ceylon (now Sri Lanka). Rules for immigrants coming to Canada under the family reunification clause, however, remained different for Europeans and Asians. Canadian residents of European origin could bring their spouse, fiancé(e), unmarried children of any age, parents, grandparents, and even orphaned nieces and nephews. People of Asian origin had to be Canadian citizens, and not merely residents, in order to sponsor family, but in their case family was restricted to spouse and unmarried children under 21 years of age.

The Immigration Act of 1952 removed the word *race* and replaced it with *ethnic group*. It incorporated the changes that had been introduced in the post-war years. Basically, the policy remained exclusionary in character by retaining the right to prohibit admission on the basis of nationality, citizenship, ethnic group, geographical area of origin, peculiar customs, unsuitability to climate, occupation, and class. Thus, the racist nature of the policy remained in keeping with majority sentiment as echoed by newspapers such as the *Toronto Star* in a 1954 editorial: "racial discrimination is an established (and most would say, sensible) feature of our immigration policy" (Walker, 1992, p. 18). A Supreme Court decision in 1955 upheld a deportation order for an Asian individual based on his race, interpreting, on the authority of the Oxford Dictionary, that the terms *race* and *ethnic group* were equivalent. West Indian domestic servants were admitted, and by 1960 their numbers rose to one thousand a year (including skilled workers). In 1956, references to Asians in immigration regulations were dropped, and selection was based on geographical areas rather than on the characteristics of applicants. In addition to Europe and Lebanon (which was considered more European than Asian), immigrants from Egypt, Israel, South and Central American countries were given preference on the grounds that, being immigrant countries themselves, it was more likely that the immigrants of European origin, rather than the local inhabitants, would want to emigrate to Canada.

After the introduction of the Bill of Rights Act in 1960, Prime Minister John Diefenbaker was able to initiate changes in immigration policy. Based on his argument that a racially exclusionary policy was neither in keeping with Canada's commitment to the ideals of freedom from discrimination and equality recognized in the Bill of Rights, nor with the United Nations principles of justice and equality, changes in 1962 established that the main criterion for selection of independent immigrants would be their skills. Immigrants under the family unification clause, however, remained subject to racial discrimination. The upsurge in people with less education from southern Europe prompted a change in the system, which was introduced in 1967. Three classes of immigrants were established: family, independent, and refugee. A point system eliminated racial criteria. Points in nine areas, including education and occupation, were to be the only criteria for selection of immigrants. Non-European immigrants were put on an equal status for the first time in Canadian immigration regulations. As a result of the substantial changes made in immigration laws, which removed racial criteria for the acceptance of immigrants, a diverse range of ethnic groups started changing the demographic picture of Canadian society. Third World immigration rose by 40 percent between 1967 and the mid-1970s. During that period, 115,000 West Indians (10 percent in the managerial, technical, or professional categories, with less than 3 percent labourers) and 90,000 people from India (14 percent in the professional, managerial, or technical categories, and 6 percent farmers) immigrated to Canada. By 1978 there were over 90,000 people of Syrian, Lebanese, Egyptian and other Arab backgrounds, a large percentage of whom were in the professional category. The shift of Canadian immigration policy from racially based to a more open one created many changes in the immigration pattern. This can be illustrated by the fact that before 1961, Europe was responsible for 90.4 percent of all immigrants, but by 1996, only 19 percent of immigrants came from there (Scott, 2001).

The period beginning with the declaration of a policy on multiculturalism by Prime Minister Pierre Trudeau in the early 1970s could be identified as the Multicultural Society phase. By the middle of that decade, an extensive public review of Canadian immigration policy was initiated through a Special Joint Committee on Immigration Policy, which produced a Green Paper. This resulted in the 1976 Immigration Act, whose salient features were family reunification, non-discrimination by removal of separate regulations, attention to refugees, and focus on Canada's socio-cultural and economic goals. The point system still emphasized education and training, but this time followed by such subjective issues as motivation, initiative, as well as occupational skills, age, employment prospects, and the ability to speak one of the two official languages. In actual numbers, the immigrant population (with potentially varying definitional possibilities) constituted 17.4 percent of the Canadian public, an increase of 14.5 percent since 1991 (Scott, 2001). That is indeed a long way from where we would have been had the country continued its non-inclusive immigration policies. In the meantime, the yearly immigration target is still hovering around the 1 percent objective that has been in place for some time now, and which falls somewhere around 250,000 people. In addition, Canada offers financial assistance to refugees, and its efforts to resolve the refugee problem on the international scene won it the Nansen Medal by the United Nations in 1986.

As expected, these changes in immigration and related policies are reshaping race and ethnic relations in Canada. At the time of Confederation in 1867, people of British and French origin constituted 92 percent of the total population. The present ethnic composition of Canadian society is heterogeneous, to the extent that about 50 percent of the total population across the country belongs to ethnic groups other than British. Even in francophone Quebec, about 25 percent of the population is made up of non-French groups. Efforts at confirming Canada as a multicultural society have been made through the Multiculturalism Policy (1971), the Canadian Human Rights Act (1977), the Charter of Rights and Freedoms (1982), and the Multicultural Act (1988).

Immigration is an area where government policy has changed, and a significant proportion of the public sees this phenomenon as a threat. Yet, if fertility remains at the present rate, after the year 2015, immigration will be an important source of population growth. The sharp decline in the birth rate after the baby boom has created a demographic deficit in Canada, having gone from 4.0 children per woman in 1959 to 2.0 at present, below the replacement level of 2.1 per woman. The decline in the fertility rate has also changed the age structure of Canadian society, so that instead of a broad base of young people, the number of middle aged and older people has been increasing at a more rapid rate since 1986. There was a sharp decrease in school enrolments in the 1980s, which resulted in school closures. Quebec's birth rate of 1.45 per woman in 1990 was one of the lowest in the industrialized world. Due to low birth rates and subsequent demographic shifts, the Canadian government reminds the citizens that at the present rate of population growth, without immigration, Canada will eventually disappear eight hundred years from now. As such, immigration is not an option for Canada: it is essential to the country's long-term existence.

DEVELOPMENT OF MULTICULTURAL POLICY AND LEGISLATION RELATED TO EQUITY ISSUES

Although the perception of Canada as a multicultural nation has been associated with immigration movements, policy initiative dealing with the changed profile was largely a result of three factors: the development of French nationalism in the province of Quebec in the early 1960s, which threatened Canadian federalism; aggressive state intervention in social policy; and the assertive demands of minority ethnocultural groups (Anderson and Frideres, 1981). It was not until the volatile political developments in Quebec that a Royal Commission on Bilingualism and Biculturalism was set up to study the French-English tensions in Quebec. The resulting four-volume report indicated a demographic transformation in which several ethnocultural groups, in addition to the French in Quebec, felt strongly about their cultures and demanded recognition. This was notwithstanding the linguistic assimilation of immigrant groups into the anglophone sector, which had resulted in English and French as the two main language groups in the country. The government had to recreate a policy on multiculturalism that recognized the new social reality. In 1971, Prime Minister Pierre Trudeau presented the nation with a new policy entitled "Bilingualism within a Multicultural Framework." It was the first official acknowledgement of the reality of pluralism in Canadian society:

> There cannot be one cultural policy for Canadians of British and French origin, another for the original peoples and yet another for all others. For although there are two official languages, there is no official culture, nor does any ethnic group take precedence over any other .... We are free to be ourselves .... It is the policy of this government ... to "safeguard" this freedom .... A policy of multiculturalism within a bilingual framework commends itself to the

government as the most suitable means of assuring the cultural freedom of Canadians.

It is interesting to note that, while the 1969 Official Languages Act made English and French the two official languages at the federal level, multiculturalism legislation was not enacted federally until 1988. Bilingualism was based upon the concept of the founding nations, implying special privileges to French and English groups because of their claim that they founded Canada, and as a result it ignored Canada's Native population. Bilingualism is applicable to federal offices across Canada. At the provincial level, eight of Canada's ten provinces are unilingually English, New Brunswick is bilingual, and Quebec is unilingually French. While Quebec is officially French, most government services, including education, are accessible in English to the anglophone community. The other provinces, which are officially English, offer similar minimal services to the French minorities there, particularly following court action in several provinces. Five provinces have officially accepted multiculturalism in education, and Quebec has its own intercultural education perspective.

Multiculturalism has been defined in various ways in Canada, and continues to be controversial. Conceptually, Smith et al. (1999) see it as an eclectic term that is generally responding to a perceived need and the concomitant accommodation of pluralism, which connotes a disavowal from cultural hegemony or group domination. As a pattern of social organization, the Canadian mosaic was thought of as complementary to political federalism when the policy of multiculturalism was announced in the early 1970s. Its aim was to legitimize the place of ethnocultural groups (along with the French and English) in Canadian society. As a political ideology, it has provided Canada with an identity, and a national distinction from the United States, where the emphasis has been on the idea as well as the practice of a melting pot, where immigrants and refugees become, culturally and linguistically, fully absorbed into the dominant Anglo American ways of life and worldview. As a policy, multiculturalism implies consensus within the rhetoric of a just society where there is to be unity within diversity. Its objectives are: first, to assist all cultural groups to develop a capacity to grow and contribute to Canada; second, to assist minority groups in overcoming cultural barriers so as to enjoy full participation in Canadian society; third, to promote intergroup relations; and fourth, to provide facilities to minority groups for language learning.

Despite the spirit as well as the practical implications of Canadian multiculturalism, the country has not achieved the expected *de facto* acceptance of ethnocultural groups. Needless to add that any *de jure* project of equal status of all such groups would, in effect, work against their equality of opportunities due to institutional inequalities. By implying consensus, the first objective has been criticized for having stripped culture of its political aspect. The second objective, aimed at reducing racial and ethnic discrimination for national unity, assumes that equality can be promoted through culture. Moreover, overcoming cultural barriers and language learning implies cultural deficiency among minority groups. The proposed compensatory programs are aimed at ethnocultural minorities. They neither require an adjustment in the dominant culture nor imply a redefinition of the national culture in order to create what may be referred to as the common space, or the third culture. The third objective, that of promoting inter-group relations, is aimed at reducing racial and ethnic tensions. However, this had been the weakest part of the policy until the establishment of the Multiculturalism Act (1988), and more recently, the Race Relations Directorate. The Multiculturalism Act (Bill C-93) builds on the equality and potentially equiticizing provisions in the Charter of Rights by focusing on the promotion of full and equal participation of all members in Canadian society. As a whole, the policy addresses minority cultures, the other, rather than both dominant and minority groups. This means tolerating minority cultures with what is essentially a patronizing attitude. It is a vehicle for state control of the agenda, the goals and the priorities of ethnocultural groups as well as the leadership in their communities through funding (Breton, 1991). As a means of creating national identity and fostering national unity (by deflecting tensions from among ethnocultural groups), its effectiveness can be questioned.

The concept of multiculturalism has changed over time, with equity and anti-discrimination measures added in recent years to widen its meaning. It has been strengthened by several policy initiatives and legislation. In its initial stages, multiculturalism was interpreted and implemented in a manner that stripped culture of its political aspect, and implied consensus within the rhetoric of a just society. Multicultural programs exposed Canadians to different cultures, and focused on supporting programs for the maintenance of culture and language of ethnocultural minority groups. The emphasis was on cultural pluralism—a cultural mosaic—rather than on participation of minority groups or equity issues. In that framework, white European ethnocultural groups were significantly more acceptable than visible minorities.

While other cultures are acceptable, people seen as belonging to other races are not. Racism is a major social problem, and as a result, the Multiculturalism Act of 1988 called on the government to foster equality and access for all Canadians. Eight of its nine principles are concerned with equity issues, and the last deals with culture. This change in interpretation of multiculturalism from a recognition of diversity to promotion of a full and equitable participation of Canadians of all origins is a crucial one. The objective of the Race Relations and Cross-Cultural Understanding Program is to eliminate racial discrimination at the individual and institutional levels. The 1986 federal Employment Equity Act involved the removal of barriers that limited the participation and life chances of women and visible minorities, as well as of Native and disabled persons.

The *Charter of Rights and Freedoms* (Canada, 1982a) improved upon previous constitutional guarantees that protected the individual rights of women and ethnic group members, and introduced legal provisions to prevent discrimination on the grounds of ethnicity or race. Multiculturalism is vaguely alluded to in Section 27: "This Charter shall be interpreted in a manner consistent with the preservation and enhancement of the multicultural heritage of Canadians" (Constitution Act, Canada, 1982). This has only adjectival relevance because it merely implies ethnocultural group rights. The Equality Rights in Section 15 of the Charter, which became law in 1985, guarantee an individual's protection against overt forms of discrimination. They permit, but do not require, protection for the collective rights of ethnic groups. Section 15(1) of the Charter prohibits discrimination based on gender and race, and Section 28 guarantees gender equality. Section 15(2) permits the establishment of affirmative action programs for women, even if they contravene section 15(1). Section 2 guarantees fundamental freedoms, also at the individual level.

Again, race and ethnicity concepts, as defined in this book, refer to any arbitrary classification of people on the basis of biological criteria, such as actual or assumed physiological and genetic differences. Ethnicity also refers to any arbitrary classification of people based on biological criteria of actual and assumed ancestry (physical distinctiveness) as well as cultural criteria such as socio-cultural heritage.

IDEOLOGICAL SHIFTS IN MULTICULTURAL THEORY IN CANADA

The subjective experiences of individual Canadians are determined by the objective organization of society through a multicultural policy.

While multiculturalism consists of an integrated set of information (policy-in-intention), to the individual it is a subjectively created reality, an experience (policy-in-experience). Translating multicultural policy in educational institutions has practical policy implications, although what students and teachers practice, and how they construct and organize the realities of everyday life, could be constructed on notions of past experiences. In addition, the implementation of multiculturalism comprises several ideological stages, which progress gradually from unequal dominant-subordinate group relationships to greater balance in the power equation. The stages can be identified in several immigrant countries (Ghosh and Tarrow, 1993) and can be associated with the developments in social theory discussed in Chapter I. In Canada, the stages can also be related to the phases in Canadian immigration history as identified above. The stages may be connected with the official objectives (policy-in-intention), which are not always shared by all interest groups in society and can, therefore, cause political and cultural disunity. Moreover, the stages are not always clear due to the dynamic nature of evolving dominant-subordinate relations in democracies. The evolution of a multicultural society in Canada may be seen to have passed through the following levels that conform to changing conceptions of multiculturalism.

The first phase was one of assimilation. Subordinate groups were expected to relinquish their own culture and identities in favour of the existing dominant mode. At this stage, society was monocultural, and the existence of other groups was implicitly denied. Traditional theories such as structural-functionalism regarded the school as providing opportunities for social mobility to all members of society through assimilation. In historical terms, this stage began with the European conquest of Canada. It included the period of Imperial Outpost, when the Native population was coerced to assimilate, and the immigrants, apart from the French people in

Quebec, consisted mainly of British people. In education, no attention was paid to the different needs of cultural groups. Differences in their learning styles and behavioural patterns were taken to be deficiencies. Difference was equated with inferiority, and the attempt was made to mould culturally different groups in the pattern of the dominant culture.

The second stage was one of adaptation. An ideology of cultural pluralism, based on the recognition of the presence in society of other small groups, made some overtures to help subordinate groups adjust to the dominant culture. The ideal to be achieved, however, remained the dominant group characteristics by which other groups were to be measured. These other groups in turn made up their deficiencies through the system in order to be admitted to dominant social institutions. In return, the dominant society acknowledged the existence of other groups, and showed an interest in their "exotic" cultures. The onus to succeed was on the minority groups. Liberal versions of traditional theories aimed at compensating deficiencies, and denied the power of racial, ethnic, and gender differences. This stage may be seen to correspond to the White Dominion phase in Canadian immigration. At this point, Asian immigrants continued to be severely restricted because they were considered non-assimilative, yet European immigrants were allowed entry into Canada with the hopes that they would be capable of adapting to British institutions. In education, this translated into compensatory programs as a means to equal educational opportunities. An interest in other groups was shown through familiarity with exotic cultures, but culture was viewed as artifact, and was seen as static, not dynamic. The study of other cultures was through a museum approach.

In the third stage, accommodation, attempts were made to accept the ethnocultural groups as subordinates within the dominant societal framework. These groups were even allowed to maintain their language and culture. This was based on a particular concept of multiculturalism that appeared to offer objective means to equalize opportunity. The effort in this phase shifted to the dominant group. However, this interpretation of multiculturalism neither resolved the existing basic conflicts in society such as racism and other forms of discrimination, nor did it change the system of inequality built into social institutions such as institutional discrimination and racism. Theoretically, the connection between knowledge and power was made, and neo-Marxist theories saw the school as perpetuating inequality in society. Historically, this corresponded with the period when Canada's vision was that of a Middle Power in the post-World War II years, when overtly racist language was dropped from immigration regulations. Racism became more subtle and invisible, and was practiced through stringent restrictive measures imposed by Canadian consulates in selected countries from which immigrants were expected. In education, this was represented by attempts at multicultural education programs such as ethnic studies, comparative religion, studies of other cultures, and heritage language programs, as well as attention to ethnic and gender representation in the curriculum.

Canadian society may be said to be now in the fourth stage, which is incorporation. This is an in-between phase that is a response by the dominant group to address the problem represented by the pluralist dilemma. As articulated by Bullivant (1981), this dilemma is how best to reconcile the contradiction between the ideal of justice in democracies and the rhetoric of tolerance by those who hold power on the one hand, with the reality of the practice of discrimination experienced by those who have no power on the other. "... [P]luralism contains the seeds of competition and even conflict over the allocation of access to social rewards and economic resources through education" (Bullivant, 1981, p. 14). This gives a stronger appearance to programs for shared participation, designed to equalize access of groups through affirmative action, equity, and equal opportunity programs, and by removing institutional barriers. This is an effort by the dominant group to channel political and economic activity of other groups into existing institutions rather than alienating them. Otherwise, they could pose a potential threat to the established order. However, while this allows individual mobility of some members of the groups, and their access to rights and powers of citizenship in democratic participation, this stage still maintains inequality because the dominant group uses its ideology to obtain the consent of the subordinate groups. Conflict theories explain social change as resulting from conflicting interests for power, wealth, and status. This is the period of Multicultural Society, when immigration criteria have been changed to non-racial standards. In education, this stage involves institutional efforts at equity programs, such as hiring more teachers from ethnocultural groups and visible minorities, and employment equity, as well as prejudice reduction strategies aimed at accepting other groups into the dominant framework.

The fifth stage, integration, is a radical departure in ideology. It involves all groups in a common effort to build society. This stage is marked by interdependence, reciprocity, and mutual enrichment. Theoretically, postmodernism, poststructuralism, and postcolonialism have posed a challenge to dominant Eurocentric meta-narratives, overarching philosophies and universal truths that happen to represent a particular gender, race, ethnicity, and class. Central to the critical pedagogy based on the above theories is the notion of ethnic diversity in which difference is part of a broader notion of educational equity and possible success for all learners (Nieto, 1992). Historically, Canadian society has not yet reached this stage, although it is guided by the Multiculturalism Act of 1988, which focuses on promoting full and equal participation of all members of Canadian society.

The purpose of education is revolutionized at this last stage: education is for empowerment. The perspective is one of intercultural education, defined as interchange and reciprocity in the total school culture—content, structure, and environment—for all involved in the education process. Here, groups come together as equals. The term *intercultural education* is taken from the Council of Europe, although in meaning it is somewhat different from the Council's use, and is not exactly as used in Quebec. The educational process involves cooperative learning through a global view of education and respect for human rights. It questions the very basis of the dominant ideology as legitimate knowledge taught in schools, and suggests the creation of knowledge that represents a different worldview, such as in anti-racist education. This implies a total reversal of the dominant-subordinate power equation. It may build upon previous educational programs, but the differences in ideology would indicate a radically different approach. For example, intercultural education (as defined here) and anti-racist education are not the next step to multicultural education, because they imply opposites in power relations. While the view of the world in multiculturalism is universalistic, in intercultural education the view is based on historical analysis in terms of race, class, and sex. In multicultural education, the curriculum is primarily based on Western values, as opposed to a curriculum that has a global orientation in intercultural education.

Idealistically, integration would represent the vision of a just society, with integration taking place amongst all groups, both majority and minority. Integration would question the very basis of the dominant ideology as legitimate knowledge, implying a total reversal of the dominant-subordinate power equation. It would create a third space, a third culture evolving from the shared experiences of people from various ethnocultural groups. Integration is far more than a juxtaposition of cultures and experiences, whether dominant or minority. It refers to a dynamic amalgam evolving out of the common experiences of dominant and minority cultures. It is represented by the word *and*. Integration involves mediation.

Ideally, a multicultural policy should lead towards this stage. Multiculturalism, even as it is evolving into a broader definition, has not as yet led to an integrated society, because it still legitimizes an exclusively Eurocentric view of the world. That it is possible for hitherto marginalized groups to have a voice in Canadian society, due to equality legislation, may indicate a move towards integration. True integration would be a radical departure in power relations, because it would involve all groups in a common effort to build society.

HISTORY OF MULTICULTURAL EDUCATION

English Canada

Although the British North America Act of 1867 and the Canada Act of 1982 guarantee a confessional system, and school boards are defined along religious and not linguistic lines, this has not posed any particular problems in English-speaking Canadian provinces. A major problem with federal multicultural policy is that it cannot be effectively implemented in education because education is a provincial responsibility, and neither legal nor political remedies are available in the absence of a substantive rights guarantee. The legal provisions (or protections) to prevent discrimination on the grounds of ethnicity or race in the Charter of Rights and Freedoms have implications for education. It is significant, however, that the multiculturalism clause for education is vague. The federal government assists multicultural programs and research in education through a department, originally set up as a Multiculturalism Directorate in 1972 under the Secretary of State. But the lack of federal control over education and provincial legislation in general has limited federal ability to influence education in this direction to any meaningful degree.

Across the country, multiculturalism has been variously interpreted in education. Notwithstanding the fact that Canada is an immigrant country, the provincial departments of education have historically had a policy of assimilation. The education of various groups in Canada has been assimilationist towards an Anglo-dominated culture, although at least a quarter of the population has been French and concentrated in Quebec. Furthermore, the country was built by immigrants from many parts of Europe and the Third World. Following consensus theories, education's role was seen as cultural transmission in the process of human capital formation, so essential for developing Canada. Within the vision of a monocultural society, it implied non-recognition or non-acceptance of cultural differences (except for the dominant English and the subordinate French) for ethnic group relations in all of Canada, including Quebec. Racial and ethnic, as well as gender and class, differences were negated in an attempt to devalue non-dominant group characteristics. The exclusion of the other was structural.

The policy of multiculturalism has been translated into very different forms throughout Canada. Saskatchewan was the first to implement this policy in 1975, and four other provinces have also endorsed it. Basically, linguistic choices regarding the medium of instruction were offered to the Ukrainian, Russian, German, Jewish, and native Cree populations in the western provinces of Alberta, Manitoba, and Saskatchewan. Nova Scotia, on the extreme east end of Canada, now has a strong policy of intercultural education, even though its long-settled black population suffered segregation in schools up until the 1950s. The two provinces distinctly ahead of the others with regard to educational reform and change in the direction of multiculturalism have been Ontario and British Columbia. Demographic compulsions lay at the root of this approach. British Columbia, in particular, has a large Asian population. Even now, a substantial ratio of Asian immigrants prefers to go there. In fact, historically, the longest record of diverse immigration is traceable to British Columbia. Regarding Ontario, not only do the bulk of immigrants go there, but currently about half its total population is made up of ethnocultural people. Possibly on account of this, Ontario is at the forefront in having had the maximum number of racist incidents. Multiculturalism as a policy was endorsed by the provincial government of Ontario in 1977, and now it has also adopted an anti-racist policy. Although largely decentralized, the Ministry of Education encourages the teaching of English as a Second Language, and focuses on bias in textbooks. Over the last thirty years, significant curriculum guidelines have evolved. Further, in 1987, a Policy on Race and Ethno-Cultural Equity was initiated. This paved the way by 1993 for the development of guidelines for antiracism and ethnocultural equity in school boards. The Education Act was amended in 1992, making it incumbent upon school boards in the province to put into practice the antiracism and ethnocultural equity policies. The response of the school boards has been a variety of policies and programs concerned with the curriculum, such as race relations and heritage languages, school and community relations, student placement, and recruitment of teachers.

Quebec: A Special Case

Approximately one quarter of Canada's population resides in Quebec. The greater part (74.5 percent) traces their lineage to French ancestry. The remainder, the non-French aggregate, comprise about 25 percent of the population, of which the visible minorities total about 8 percent. A small fraction, about 4 percent, are of British stock, a mere 1 percent survive from the First Nations, and the remaining 20 percent are composed of diverse ethnic groups. Until the 1960s and the Quiet Revolution, the policy of the provincial government of Quebec, led by Maurice Duplessis, was to discourage immigration, lest the unique nature of French Quebec be threatened. As per the British North America Act, until 1967 both federal and provincial governments jointly administered immigration policies. The change in attitude towards immigration came about in Quebec due to a significant decline in the birthrate. To facilitate faster immigration, the Quebec government requested more autonomy in the selection of immigrants. This was acceded to in 1991, as per the McDougall Gagnon-Tremblay agreement. Quebec is currently the only province that has its own immigration department.

It was inevitable that in a French majority region, the continuance of English—the dominant language in social, political, and economic spheres—would one day result in the emergence of a powerful French nationalism. By the 1960s, this trend manifested itself in a rejection by the French not only of bilingualism, but of multiculturalism as well. This was known as the Quiet Revolution, distinctively expressed by some elements of the francophone elite in the phrase *maîtres chez nous* (masters of our own house), which also resulted in a significant growth of the educational system. The idea was to challenge anglophone supremacy in an attempt to end the discrimination—both ethnic and linguistic—that had affected French Canadians on their own terrain. The French in Quebec required more than bilingualism as an instrument to augment their socio-economic status and power, although it certainly had symbolic value for the survival of French in the rest of Canada.

The policy of multiculturalism, by implying equal status for all cultures, further diluted the attempt at French cultural revitalization. At a time of fervent francization, the classification of French culture as being equal in status to other cultures in federal multiculturalism policy was unacceptable. This was especially so because English language and culture would undoubtedly emerge at the top in a continent that is predominantly English. The rise of French nationalism was an offshoot of the reality that French Canadians comprise a mere two percent of the North American population. The problem of higher educational and employment opportunities in a continent where 98 percent use English is cause for great anxiety to those communities who fear being progressively cut off from the larger continental base. Their concern for survival by maintaining a distinctive identity—linguistic, social, and cultural—prompted legislation to safeguard their language as a first step. French became the official language of Quebec in 1974. Bill 101 in 1977 went a step further, making it obligatory for all children, except those having English parents educated in English in Canada, to be taught in French. This was a controversial piece of legislation, as it gave the priority to the rights of francophones as a collectivity over the individual rights of non-francophones with certain far-reaching repercussions.

Accepting that the medium of instruction should be French, *La Politique québécoise du développement culturel* spelled out the policy of the Quebec Government in 1978 concerning the importance of diversity in constructing a common society through the medium of the French language. In 1990, the Quebec government made a major statement with regard to immigration in acknowledgement of the pluralistic challenges latent within its society. Several salient factors led to this official endorsement: the continuous demographic decline of the French population (the prevalent fertility rate of 1.45 was certain to decimate future generations, a possibility further aggravated by substantial outmigration); a significant increase in the aging of the population (current estimates are that 25 percent of the population will exceed 65 years of age in another decade); and the need to give a stimulus to the economy through expansion of the labour market and increased consumption (the relation between unemployment and migration is inverse). Congruent upon this, large numbers of non-French, mostly non-white, groups arrived in Quebec, posing a serious threat to the French language. To safeguard French interests, the government document of 1990 had three main objectives: (a) facilitating easy access to French language teaching; (b) fostering a sense of belonging and participation amongst immigrant and ethnic groups; and (c) developing inter-group relations among all residents of Quebec. Broadly, these aims resemble the federal multicultural policy.

It is ironic that francization is occurring precisely at a time when the immigration of various other cultural groups (notably Vietnamese, Haitian, Latin American, and Lebanese) has of necessity become significant. The threat to French language and culture, due to the sharp decline in birthrate and the need to offset it through immigration, poses a psychological threat at a time of French cultural revitalization. On the other hand, the need for even stronger programs of francization would be a response to the challenge of the influx of non-French groups—most of them non-white—into Quebec society. Immigrants are increasingly seen as posing a threat to the survival of the French language.

Intercultural Education in Quebec

Quebec took the initiative and became the first of the provinces in Canada to offer legal guarantees for the educational rights of minorities through its Charter of Rights in 1975. Several more years elapsed, however, before the educational, social, and cultural needs of the non-French groups that had settled in Quebec could be focused upon. The objective of *Autant de façons d'être Québécois: plan d'action du Gouvernement du Québec à l'intention des communautés culturelles* (1981) was to eliminate all forms of discrimination for members of cultural communities and work towards their right to equal opportunity. This was reinforced by documents relating to cultural communities and immigration, in 1981 and 1985. However, the needs of new Quebecers are being dealt with through a Ministry of Cultural Communities and Immigration (MCCI), which was established in 1981. Intercultural education was to be the formula for enabling the integration of new arrivals, though a formal intercultural education policy had not been enunciated. A special advisory body of the MCCI was to proffer guidance concerning equal opportunity for the various ethnic and cultural groups. Furthermore, in tandem with the Ministry of Education's department (*Direction des Services Educatifs aux Communautés Culturelles*), more programs in consonance with the philosophy of integration have been developed. Interculturalism means a Quebec that will be pluralistic in outlook but francophonic through the medium of the French language.

In fact, the overall policy of education and learning among groups in Quebec has to respond, at least officially, to new efforts to "integrate immigrant students and prepare the whole student population to participate in social interaction in democratic, Francophone, pluralistic Quebec" (Quebec, 1998b, p. v). This call for a pluralistic, but again francophone, situation may not satisfy the needs of a fully implemented, critical inter-culturalism or even situationally effective inter-cultural education, but the supremacy of the French language, even if and when all other items on the agenda are theoretically equal, is apparently not open for discussion.

In its 1998 policy document, the government exhorts "[a]ll educational institutions, including vocational and adult education centres and colleges [to] conform to the basic school regulations respecting educational services in Quebec" that should sustain and advance the continuing francization of what it sees as a multi-ethnic Quebec (Quebec, 1998b, p. 4). In its *Plan of Action 1998–2002* (Quebec, 1998b, p. 9), the government also instructs all CEGEPs (two- to three-year post-secondary colleges) to "promote the teaching profession among young people enroled in the social sciences, particularly students from other backgrounds. The universities, in the framework of their policy of accommodating diversity, will make special efforts to increase the number of immigrant students or students born of immigrant parents in the faculties of education." With these new visions, the government also affirms that "although students in the education system come from many backgrounds, speak different languages and hold various religious beliefs, they must master the elements of a common framework of learning and acquire a common set of values" (Quebec, 1998b, p. 5).

The observational simplicity as well as the intended benignancy of this last statement for a more cooperative learning and intercultural environment is quite clear. What may transmit a certain degree of ambiguity in the new setting, though, is that the different backgrounds, languages, and religions may base their relational experiences on certain values that could not always be congruent with the structures and contents of the French/francophone milieu. But again, policy-makers are without a doubt aware of this fact, and at the end of the day, the francophone element must override all others for the good of French Quebec in an overwhelmingly anglophone North America. The French language, therefore, is not only a utilitarian or selectively educational language in this context, but also the *sine qua non* of Quebec's cultural survival, and must be presented in a positive light by schools and other learning institutions (Quebec, 1998b). This point on the French language was stipulated very clearly in the 1998 policy document:

"Priority should be given to providing all students with a positive image of French. Their active participation in Québec's cultural, economic and political development will be shaped by their image of the language. Access to the culture, which is inherent in a knowledge of the language, is often left out of teaching practices. This reflects a tendency to see the language purely as a subject to be taught. In addition to its functional aspects, language is a vehicle of culture and thought, and a sphere of creativity"(Quebec, 1998a, p. 25).

The emotional tendencies of the above statement aside, it is situationally practical to suspect the power of the French language to shape people's perceptions outside of French-speaking territories. That should be so with the current globalization of business and political transactions, where the overall picture is now extensively of universalized English that is relentlessly establishing itself as the lingua franca of our world. Despite these facts, though, it will be difficult to not comprehend the emotional attachment that is at work in French Canada, where the continued prominence of the French language is to be legislated, safeguarded, and vigorously promoted.

Previously, the significant, even pivotal, role of language in intercultural school programs came out clearly in the report published by the Committee on Quebec Schools and Cultural Communities in 1985. Three kinds of programs have been envisaged by the government to assist in the integration of students. The first is orientation and welcoming classes (*classes d'accueil*) for newcomers, with the objective of imbibing French language skills, which have been in vogue since 1969. The second program, operated through *centres d'orientation et de formation des immigrants* (COFI), is intended for adults and structured to equip them with a working knowledge of French, falling short of the level required to take courses in the language. The goal of the last program is to safeguard heritage languages through PELO (*programme d'enseignement des langues d'origine*). These are publicly funded (up to 80 percent) but privately managed ethnic schools for the preservation of ancient languages of the land. However, the criticism of these schools is that they are insular and segregationist in nature, and not nearly good enough as a substitute for learning in English. In the case of COFI, it is clear from the experiences of many who attended them that its programs are so limited that most learners come out of them without any tangible capacities to function in French. And without any automatically available, government-funded intermediate or advanced courses, many wonder how any effective linguistic integration of adult immigrants and refugees could take place in Quebec.

In the case of PELO on the other hand, McAndrew (cited in Smith et al., 1999) points out that the premium many allophones are placing on ethnic languages may be diminishing vis-à-vis French (or English) precisely because of the utilitarian disadvantages associated with ethnic vernaculars in Canada. McAndrew adds that "PELO is often promoted more in French schools as a means to encourage better transition to using French and integrating into the school community than in fostering cultural pluralism" (Smith et al., 1999, p. 353). That is indeed the case, for French students are not required to learn about the cultures or the languages of so-called ethnics. So PELO, in its entirety, especially when one takes into account the limited instruction it involves, may simply serve as a temporary self-esteem booster during the transition into one of the dominant languages.

It is probably as a result of this inadequacy in integration and language training that new policies (Quebec, 1997) are directed at giving new and immigrant students effective and more comprehensive access to the acquisition of the necessary tools—language training, cultural information, reliable progress assessment, etc.—for educational success. Policy documents actually recognize the educational problems recent immigrants are facing in Quebec, with the clear warning that if these groups are not given the special need and support they require, they many never graduate (Quebec, 1998a). Among the items proposed in this regard is the allocation of new and effective remedial resources, as well as involving parents and other community organisations in the education of newly arrived learners.

It has been pointed out (McAndrew, 1985) that the tendency to see themselves as victims of linguistic menace makes French Canadians systematically neglect problems faced by new immigrant groups. Cultural communities find themselves caught between the two solitudes. That may not be healthy for learning purposes, as these groups, because they either have to speak and act English or French, could in effect come down with an acute case of cultural alienation. And that is, if anything, pointedly antithetical to the spirit of Canada's multiculturalism and Quebec's inter-cultural education. Pedagogically at least, as McLaren (1997, p. 16) reminds us, "language provides the self-definitions upon which people act, negotiate various subject positions, and undertake a process of naming and renaming the relations between themselves, others, and the world." In addition, writes Giroux,

> If language is inseparable from lived experience and from how people create a distinctive voice, it is also connected to an intense struggle among different groups over what will count as meaningful and whose cultural capital will prevail in legitimating particular ways of life. Within schools, discourse produces and legitimates configurations of time, space, and narrative, placing particular renderings of ideology, behaviour, and the representation of everyday life in a privileged perspective. As a "technology of power", discourse is given concrete expression in the forms of knowledge that constitute the hidden curriculum of schooling (1997, p. 121).

While McLaren and Giroux speak about certain educational problematics that could be extrapolated to the possible ramifications of imposing French on non-francophones living in Quebec, and selectively highlight the need for a conscientious awareness about the potential weight native languages carry in facilitating or hindering life possibilities for many learners here and elsewhere, they should not still propose, in the current configuration of the Canadian public space, the dilution of French as the medium of instruction in Quebec schools. The reasons for this last observation should be self-explanatory: the cultural survival argument in the North American context has to be taken seriously; in addition, the dual language policy is still intact, with English serving as the major medium of instruction outside of Quebec.

Again, despite the non-negotiable status of French, there are other initiatives in Quebec that are proposed to decrease the educational and cultural burdens on new immigrants. These include increasing cultural community representation in curriculum material, hiring of minority staff, and as mentioned above, development of school-community relations. In highlighting this last point, the policy document (Quebec, 1998a, p. 23) emphasizes how "educational institutions must involve the parents more in various aspects of school life, consult them, and inform them about Québec's education system, [and] the school culture." While these are important points in school situations, it is also essential to realize the educational, linguistic, and cultural difficulties immigrant or refugee parents could face in these new, sometimes complex and often alienating, situations. It is more common that these parents who do not speak the school language are generally unemployed, and often come from traditions where teachers and principals are not questioned about the state of the students. While overcoming all these is not easy, the school's attitude towards these selectively powerless parents, or even communities, may not always be encouraging. So the task to ameliorate the situation for immigrant or refugee pupils, their parents and their ethnic groups requires more focus, more resources, and more recognition than have been hitherto allocated, especially as the population ratio of school age allophones increases. Currently, the Ministry of Education is only planning to "study and, if necessary, review adult education services, especially for parents of immigrant students, in the context of public education support programs in order to help these parents with the integration of their children into the Québec school system" (Quebec, 1998b, p. 6). While that program, if it is ever implemented, will be too late for tens of thousands of immigrant and refugee parents, it will, nevertheless, be an important step in the right direction. The incorporation of these parents as important stakeholders in the Quebec educational situation is crucial and long overdue, to say the least, and could not have come sooner.

One step among the many that are needed was taken some years back, when the Ministry of Education began intercultural training programs for educational personnel. The Ministry of Higher Education and Sciences also supports some training initiatives for CEGEP teachers in Montreal. However, the emphasis is not on discrimination, and equality issues and anti-racist education are not proposed by any school board. This may reveal the symbolic face of the two government bodies' policy approach. The fact will still remain, however, that until such issues as rampant but hard to prove discrimination—and, therefore, the acute need for anti-racist education—are addressed, the current band-aid approach will simply cover educational problems that will be more cumbersome, and definitely socially more expensive, to deal with in the coming years and decades.

Given Quebec's history, it was perhaps unavoidable that the socio-political discourse would centre mainly on the French-English equation. Issues relating to the urgent needs of cultural communities that make up Quebec society have been dealt with only within the context of Quebec nationalism, rather than on their own merit, and have focused primarily on language. The lack of a formal policy is significant, and programs for intercultural education are aimed at specific services for cultural community students. More than 25 years after Bill 101, with the evolution in the identity of French-Canadians to Quebecers of French Canadian ancestry and majority status in the province (McAndrew, 1993), the focus must move beyond compensatory measures. Still, the need to be educated in French in Quebec may hardly be questioned when the fact of English education is not challenged in English Canada. Until this is recognized, though, the attempts at intercultural education will remain peripheral to language learning (Ghosh et al., 1995). Language learning is a necessary but not sufficient condition to enhancing intercultural education. A museum approach would be reductionist, since it deals with the learning of cultures as artifacts stripped of their political connotations. The basic equality needs of cultural communities still occupy a low priority in Quebec education and society. This is evident from the persistence of a non-inclusive "we" that gives ethnic students the feeling of not belonging to the Quebec community, resulting in inter-ethnic isolation. This "we" does nothing to bolster an important tenet of Quebec education, which is "the promotion and implementation of education for citizenship, where the result is the active and free participation of all citizens in the province's socio-economic and political life" (Quebec, 1998a). That could be so, for a productive cultural life for all necessitates, as Giroux (1997, p. 140) notes, "a pedagogy [...] that is attentive to the histories, dreams, and experiences that [all] students bring to school." Hence, the need, even at the most general policy level, to appreciate the values, experiential and aspirational spaces upon which so many students in Quebec would situate themselves.

Moreover, the racist nature of some curriculum material, and the lack of participation of parents of other communities in school activities, are other instances that are educationally detrimental, although considerable progress has been made in each of these areas (McAndrew, 1993). Again, the achievement of even the selective equality that forms the core of Quebec's interculturalism and inter-cultural education where "the best way to bolster the students' sense of belonging and solidarity is by fostering their active participation in the development and enrichment of Quebec's collective heritage" (see Quebec, 1998a, p. 26) may be jeopardized unless both the policy momentum and material investment are greatly increased and effectively connect the linguistic, cultural and, therefore prevalent, scholastic attachment and achievement gaps. With this concise but relatively comprehensive discussion of the Quebec situation, let us shift the focus towards the state of Aboriginal education.

THE SPECIAL SITUATION OF THE EDUCATION OF CANADA'S ABORIGINALS

The inroads made by occidental culture and values have caused incalculable damage and suffering to the psyche and spirit of the original inhabitants of Canada, referred to as Aboriginals, or people of First Nations. They became the target and victims of mass-scale racism, discrimination, and overall marginalization at the hands of the majority group. Far worse, the educational system thrust upon them wrought havoc on almost all aspects of their lives by disorienting their ways of living and, in the process, disturbing their inner harmony and balanced relationship with their environment. The continuously alienating programs of education were especially a major factor in their current plight, which includes a very high rate of under-education, unemployment, indigence, alcoholism, and related mental disorders, as well as a youth suicide rate that is sometimes estimated at 10 times the national average.

These negative and painful experiences were largely the consequence of an insensitive and callous educational approach. A new and culturally enlightened policy is the key to a transformation that would help these people integrate as equal partners in Canadian society. Evidently, to achieve this, a distinct paradigm shift in all the educational and economic development structures of the Native people is required. The conventional perspective that viewed the socio-cultural matrix of the Aboriginal as retrograde must change drastically. Rather, the intrinsic elements of Aboriginal culture must be utilized to lay a strong foundation for building a strong self-image and an optimistic vision of the future.

Long before the advent of Europeans in Canada, the Native people had been organized as nations. They had their own separate political identities. However, they were perforce subjugated with a series of treaties with the colonizers, which resulted in their political marginalization, the usurpation of their lands, and their subsequent and continuing displacement. In these organized programs of colonization and subordination, the peoples of First Nations were thrust out of their traditional lands and placed in reservations. Their territorial rights were constricted to the discussion of these geographic reservations. The combined forces of these schemes of physical and psychological deprivation denied the Native people any meaningful control of their lives and their socio-political structures, as well as other institutions.

The Aboriginal population of Canada does not identify itself with those groups of Canadians referred to as ethnic. Although they are perhaps the greatest victims of racism, it is a fact that they are not immigrants; nor do they regard themselves as visible minorities. Rather, being the originals they consider themselves to be of higher status—"citizens plus," so to speak—and they feel that their rights should be more substantial than those granted to other groups. They state their claims in a manner similar to the way negotiations between nations take place. Historically, it is undeniable that their lineage can be traced back over millennia, as far back as nine thousand years in the case of the Innu of Labrador. Unquestionably, they are Canada's First Nations, comprising well over 550 Indian, Métis, and Inuit groups. It seems that the work of the Assembly of First Nations (AFN) would enhance new possibilities for a unified platform and collective voice for raising the awareness of Aboriginals' historical rights needs, and would raise the needed awareness and action for their cultural, political, and socio-economic concerns.

There was a time during the 17th century when Native people

enjoyed equal status with the French as trading partners. The French were just establishing their settlements in the area surrounding the St. Lawrence River, and the single most important item of trade was fur. This status as a commercial partner changed gradually for the Aboriginals, because they came to be regarded as a stumbling block to the colonialists' expansionist plans. As a result, the Native groups became confined in limited spaces known as reservations. Zealous missionaries performed their appointed role in converting the Native Indians to Christianity and indoctrinating them into Euro-Canadian norms. The goal was to assimilate the Natives so that they would pose no threat to the expansionist plans of the colonizers.

France, however, did not have a policy of land transfers, and this has led to the issue of land claims in recent times. With the transfer of New France to Britain, a Royal Proclamation in 1763 led to the surrender of Aboriginal rights over vast territories. At Confederation, the British North America Act of 1867 (Section 91) gave the government of Canada the exclusive right to make laws for "Indians, and Lands reserved for the Indians." The Inuit were not mentioned at that time. In 1939, a Supreme Court decision defined Eskimos as Indians. While this made them part of the British North America Act, it did not give them treaty settlements with the government, and later caused problems with land claims. Status or treaty Indians, on the other hand, claim that their treaty provisions have not been fulfilled by the government. The Constitutional Act of 1982 (Section 35) contains three sections on Aboriginal peoples of Canada, which includes Indians, Inuit, and Métis. The definition of *Indian* has changed over the years, and the parliament of Canada is free to define *Indian*, which it currently does as simply a person who is registered as an Indian.

The day-to-day relationship between the Indians and the government is controlled by the Indian Act, an act of parliament that has changed over the years, with the last major revision coming in 1961.

Bill C-31 (1985) reinstated the legal status of about 136,512 First Nations peoples across the country. However, several Aboriginal groups do not fall under the Indian Act and are non-status, which means that they are not officially entitled to the Aboriginal rights enshrined in the Canadian Constitution. For example, when Newfoundland entered the Confederation in 1949, the Aboriginal populations within the territory of Newfoundland and Labrador were not considered different from the other inhabitants and, consequently, now do not have special rights. Indian status is largely inherited, but it is quite possible for a registered or status Indian to have no Indian blood. In addition, an Indian need not be a Canadian citizen. The Métis, for example, trace their heritage to the Scottish and French settlers and Aboriginal women, and some are still struggling for official status and recognition as distinct from other indigenous groups.

THE EVOLUTION OF NATIVE EDUCATION IN CANADA

The most powerful vehicle for the achievement of assimilation of the original inhabitants of Canada in the nineteenth century was education. The target group was the young impressionable generation, who were more likely to absorb and accept the Christian, European, and capitalist ethos. The educational content was structured in such a manner as to denigrate the society and culture of the First Nations and to make the Native children forget their heritage and history as free nations. The way was thus clear for them to assume the trappings of the colonizers. As Scott (quoted in Archibald, 1995, p. 348) notes, "the great forces of intermarriage and education will finally overcome the lingering traces of native custom and tradition." This pressure to assimilate—or as Marie Battiste (1998) calls it, organized cognitive imperialism—did not lead to integration. Rather, it led to the quasi-permanent creation of an acutely underdeveloped underclass that is shaped, at least for the most part, by the direct result of redefining them as culturally deprived. In schooling, as in society, inequalities meted out to them kept the Native population in their underprivileged position.

Education is a special case in the Indian Act. An Indian child must attend school between the ages of seven and sixteen. The education of non-status Indians and Métis was neglected for decades because of the confusion between provincial/territorial and federal governments over jurisdiction and responsibility. For status Indians, after Confederation in 1867, assimilation policy was better organized through residential schools. The industrial residential schools were administered by the federal Department of Indian Affairs and several religious denominations. These schools were located far off to avoid contact with parents, and children were sent away for 10 or more months in the year. Native languages and cultures were stifled. Rudimentary academic subjects were taught, but the emphasis was on trade skills for boys and domestic science for girls. In addition, the schools were overcrowded and riddled with disease and numerous other problems.

Parents initially cooperated with these institutions in the hope that they would equip and enable their children to cope with the new way of life. But as they became disillusioned and pained by long separations, disease, and death, parents became hostile. It was evident that their values and beliefs were being undermined, their children had become strangers and the family unit was being destroyed. Adult values, based on a totally different social structure, found the schools cruel and the disciplinary regime exploitative of children's labour. It was obvious that children's achievements remained at low grade levels and led to low-skilled jobs. Most of all, Native children were neither part of the Euro-Canadian life nor comfortable with their parents' life. Nor were they able to compete in the dominant society or prepared for life in the reserves. This induced parents to demand schools on their reserves, resulting in the establishment of day schools. But lack of qualified teachers and appropriate curricula resulted in low quality schools.

After World War II, there was a shift in the policy on Indian education. Financial problems led to a policy of integration, which meant Native children would attend public schools (as opposed to segregated Indian schools) and were to be treated the same way as other children. This was done through an amendment in the Indian Act whereby provinces were to take over Native education, although the federal government maintained financial responsibility. The underlying objective, however, remained the assimilation of Indians through formal education.

The history of education of the Native population by missionaries and the governments is one of a clash of cultural values. The differences are basic, and stem from Native perceptions of harmony with nature, community, and collaborative orientation, in opposition to the dominant group values of exploitation and control of nature, and competition within a capitalistic and individualistic orientation. Native people have a special relationship with the land, and their identity and self-respect are linked to that relationship. They have highly developed community and group values of cooperation, respect, and importance given to elders, and an oral tradition of sharing their cultural heritage. Today their education is a struggle to maintain their heritage and survive as distinct people, just as their ancestors struggled to survive colonization and occupation. However, the significant changes in their way of living as part of a modern society, and the development of the north where non-Native practices have displaced traditional ways of life, pose challenges to an education in which Native and non-Native groups must learn to respect reciprocal rights and freedoms.

With increasing immigration, the assimilationist educational policy towards Indians and immigrants was challenged. The Multiculturalism Policy was not accepted by the Native groups, as the policy ignores their treaty and Aboriginal rights. Initially, the translation of multicultural policy meant a move from assimilation to adaptation, and compensatory programs were aimed at what was considered missing from the perspective of the majority Euro-Canadian culture. Although they were found lacking in modern Canadian values, Native cultures were studied as artifacts. With the period of accommodation, general curricula material was examined for stereotypes. Several large studies indicated the extent to which Native peoples had been stereotyped, and occasionally romanticized, in written and pictorial material in textbooks, and portrayed as backward, lazy, cruel, unscientific, superstitious, dirty, and alcoholic. Moreover, historical facts had been distorted and given interpretations to suit the colonizers. This led to changes in textbooks to a more accurate portrayal of Native history and culture, with more school time designated to learning about Canada's original peoples.

In contemporary Canada, the relationship of First Nations groups with the government is dramatically different. After a long history of neglect of non-status Indian and Métis education that led to their marginalization, the provincial governments and territories have now assumed responsibility in that area. Ironically, the Native leaders, themselves products of the assimilationist educational policy of the government, are the agents who have mobilized and politicized their groups to challenge their subjugation. The National Indian Brotherhood has, for example, identified self-determination as the only way to break the cycle of poverty and dependency. Their demand for Indian control of Indian education was accepted by the federal government in 1973. A response to problems identified by provincial groups of First Nations peoples across Canada, the policy involves greater community control in administration and curricula content and pedagogy, more parental involvement, increase in trained First

Nations teachers, and training in Native culture for non-Native teachers through pre-service and in-service courses (Archibald, 1995). This active involvement of First Nations people in curriculum development and control of education, exemplified by the relatively successful experiments undertaken by, among other groups, the Mi'Kmaq of Nova Scotia and the Cree people of Northern Quebec, is considered essential to making Native children proud of their heritage, and to develop self confidence in an effort to reverse their situation, which is at the bottom of the vertical mosaic. It is also essential to breaking the mutual distrust between the First Nations and the government that has developed over centuries.

It is evident that Native empowerment will come only with First Nations people's ownership of institutions that affect their lives, and education is perhaps the most important of them. To reverse the legacy of loss of control of their land, socio-cultural institutions, and languages, their minimal demand is and must be the control of educational institutions (Battiste, 1998; Kirkness, 1998). The development of locally controlled schools in the reserves is not without challenges, such as lack of qualified First Nations teachers and curricula material. This is an important educational objective that is promoted by the Assembly of First Nations, which says that "the promotion of community based and governed education systems through treaty and Aboriginal rights" with the objective of achieving First Nations jurisdiction over education is essential (AFN, 2002). Again, the question of the substantial number of Native students in the public schools (about 50 percent of Native children) in urban Canadian centres is likely to remain unresolved for some time. Power sharing at the board level and increased Native culture and history in the regular curriculum seem to be immediate possibilities for developing respect and cooperation in the multicultural milieu of urban schools. In that way, the racism to which Native and visible minority children alike are potentially subjected will have to be dealt with through the regular channels. In all, the project of recasting and recreating Native education for cultural revival and viable social development constitutes, in Marie Battiste's characterization, "a complex arrangement of conscientization, resistance, and transformative praxis that seeks to transform the dual crises related to colonization and culture" (Battiste, 2000, p. xxi).

CONCLUSION

At its birth, the Canadian state defined its relationship with Native groups through the Indian Act of 1876, which institutionalized discrimination towards the Aboriginal populations. Later, bio-cultural characteristics were used to justify discrimination against the Chinese, South Asian, Ukrainian, and Jewish Canadians. Racist and sexist immigration policies, which favoured Europeans over Third World immigrants, helped to categorize Canadian society along racial and ethnic lines. Quebec, which recently acquired extraordinary power to select its own immigrants, has a preference for French-speaking people, first from European countries, and then from Africa and Asia. Here the linguistic factor is added to race and ethnicity.

As a country, Canada has an ongoing challenge in the immediate future to solve its constitutional crisis. The claims of Quebec for special status or sovereignty and the rights of Canada's First Nations would not probably be resolved. The language question in Quebec is perhaps one of the thorniest issues. Although Canada has been officially bilingual since the early 1970s, historically English has been the language for social and economic mobility, even in French Canada (until language legislation in 1977, which had and has tremendous implications for the education of non-English and non-French cultural groups). While immigration policy prior to 1967 preferred

European immigration, and four-fifths of immigrants came from Europe, now almost three-quarters are visible minorities. The education of their children, with implications for employment without discrimination, will be a major issue as these groups become politically organized.

Multiculturalism, as interpreted in education, began from a view of culture as artifact, and was limited to a static version that stripped multicultural education programs of their political content. On the other hand, education policy in Quebec recognizes the fundamental function of the schools as being highly political institutions, and language legislation in this province is an obvious instrument in educational politics. Both multicultural and intercultural education, as practiced in different parts of Canada, fit the cultural politics of modernism, liberal ideology, and consensus theory, and are at the transitory stage between accommodation and incorporation. Both policies continue to reproduce the dominant culture through education. As a matter of fact, this is explicitly stated in Quebec as a significant means of francization. What distinguishes this stage from previous ones is the liberal rhetoric and the educational programs that attempt to accommodate the needs of other groups. The need to make an effort to include hitherto excluded groups has been recognized through compensatory programs and minority language and culture programs. For example, English as a second language and French language courses were expected to make up deficiencies among culturally different students. Despite this attempt, education was still based on unequal relations between the anglophones and the allophones, and the francophones and the allophones.

The multiculturalism policy, by focusing on a depoliticized version of culture, gave mostly symbolic power to other ethnic groups. In Quebec, although the language issue is highly politicized, intercultural programs have tended to be stripped of political content. Intercultural policy is not formalized in the same way as language legislation. But intercultural education, like multicultural policy, provides symbolic power to the cultural communities. However, symbolic power simply ends up reinforcing dominant relations in society when it is not translated into political power.

Both in anglophone and francophone Canada, education may be thought to be at the accommodation stage. Multicultural and intercultural policies in education are alike in implying the centrality of the dominant culture while extending facilities to other ethnic groups to integrate. Both policies emphasize language learning: multiculturalism by providing facilities to learn the two official languages, and interculturalism in terms of French in Quebec where Bill 101 has shown dramatic success in making French the *lingua franca*. Language is undoubtedly a basic need for students, both majority and minority, empowering them with the skills to master their own destiny. However, it is well-documented that students face problems of discrimination in access and treatment, and racism because of cultural and racial differences (even when they know the language) in anglophone as well as francophone school systems. For example, black French-speaking students face racism in the French Quebec school system as much as black West Indian students do in the English system in other parts of Canada. The isolating factor here is race. From the point of view of critical pedagogy, the notion of culture in education has been abstracted from the concepts of power and conflict rather than seen in its dialectical relationship with the socio-economic/political structure.

In the multicultural model, the response of subordinate groups is to conform to the dominant society. However, it is in fact impossible for some groups such as visible minorities to gain membership in the two dominant groups. Another possible response is that a minority group may resist the dominant group ideology and develop on its own to challenge the position of dominance. Although this has been Quebec's response as a province, within it, other subordinate groups are expected to conform.

The multicultural reality is significant for schools, because educational institutions are responsible for preparing all students to participate fully in a multicultural society. A multicultural policy that only helps students retain their cultural identities may be seem to satisfy the groups, but it neither develops a sense of nationhood nor gives them the skills, knowledge or power to control their destinies in the creation of, and participation in, a just society. A redefined multicultural education is one that would not only engage in human rights concepts, but would go so far as to question existing social structures and institutions in the context of social relations of gender, race, and class.

The equality provisions in the Multicultural Bill (1988) and other legislation, and the anti-racist initiatives in Ontario and British Columbia, have focused action away from compensatory programs within the overall structure of dominant ideology to incorporate the subordinate groups as part of the common language and cultural capital in the educative process. A critical and redefined multicultural education would change the culture of the schools. The true test of multicultural and intercultural education will be evident only through the changes in inequities of wealth and power, which currently reflect an ethnic hierarchy both in Quebec and the larger Canadian society.

Since multicultural policy has been in effect for the last 33 years (as of 2004), its impact upon Canadian society must be said to be negligible in terms of affecting equality. While multicultural and intercultural education programs theoretically give equal access to all ethnocultural groups, they have not resulted in equal participation in the educational or the economic sphere. The definition of knowledge and learning, as well as the cultural capital and language codes of a dominant culture, make academic success particularly difficult for those who do not belong (Apple, 1999, 2000). Different socio-cultural positions transmit different worldviews, and some are more powerful than others. With today's rapidly globalizing and highly immigrant world society—an issue treated in the next chapter, which focuses on education and the globalization of difference—Canadians cannot afford to ignore the implications of a failed multicultural policy, and now face the challenge of redefining its meaning in the quest for peace and collective prosperity.

4 | EDUCATION AND THE GLOBALIZATION OF DIFFERENCE WITH REFERENCE TO THE POST-SEPTEMBER 11 WORLD

> *There are at least four things we should not do as a response to the events of September 11th. We should not confuse patriotism with nationalism; we should not succumb to simplistic binaries; we should not compromise our civil liberties for a perceived sense of safety; and we should not pretend that we have changed.*

> —*Gloria Ladson-Billings*

THEORETICAL DISCUSSIONS

While the systematic and disciplinary study of globalization may be relatively new, the international, indeed inter-continental, movement of people, commerce, cultures, and ideas have been as old as the formation of societies and other territory-based human formations. In recorded history, one must accept that all universalist religions, early Greek and Roman Empire wars, and territorial and dynastic shifts in Asia, Africa, and pre-Columbus America were all, in one important way or another, select components of globalization. Needless to add that the so-called European explorers were fully engaged in a Eurocentric and, therefore, hegemonic form of globalization, that has, with some European countries becoming the centre of the world, facilitated the subsequent and arguably one of the most pervasive forms of globalization: colonialism and the physical, as well as the psychological, colonization of the non-European people of the world. In fact, because colonialism has done so much, in terms of material wealth and highly enduring psychological gains for Europeans, current programs of globalization may be inherently linked to that in more than one way.

With the general idea, as well as select practice, of globalization essentially with us for so long, current themes and programs of globalization may be seen as qualitatively different from anything humanity has seen before in two important ways. First, the new globalization does not explicitly aim, even if results are sometimes problematic, for the territorial conquest or the religious conversion of people, lands and countries. Second, globalization presents itself as primarily economic, or as McLaren puts it (1998, p. 431), "the cannibalization of the social and political by the economy," and trade-oriented with the free, cross-boundaries movement of goods and services hailed as an almost sacrosanct project that would lead to better possibilities for all (Williamson, 1993). As such, present-day globalization not only connotes that political and economic barriers are going down, but that the process must be normalized and welcomed by all, for it is, even from pure ideological perspective, something that is good. Here, though, the point must be again nuanced, for as Gibbins and Youngman (1996) note, the aim is not to completely eliminate— whether at the national or global level—social and political differences, but to telescope them so as to diminish their incompatibility and enhance their co-functionality.

Also inherent in the multi-located theses of globalization is the creation of a world where the nation-state becomes subservient to the demands of international markets, and where, because it has hastily and impractically assumed that liberal democracy is the cure for all our political ailments (see Fukuyama, 1992), all countries would eventually obey the laws of universal monoeconomics. As Stromquist (2002) notes, this new globalization has new dimensions both in form and in intensity, and due to the prevalence of individualism and open competition in all aspects of people's lives, therefore, little space is preserved for critical and progressive thought. In addition, one might also see that at least philosophically, globalization is advancing a thematically significant but politically suppressed notion of the survival of the fittest that could marginalize those who may be less competitive in the global theatre of operations. But again, since one cannot call for a timeout in the course of the game of globalization, those who may be jeopardized by their difference from the mainstream in societies where they are minorities, must incessantly, it must be said, use one of the best weapons available, i.e., education, to move, as much as possible, to the relativized politico-cultural and socio-economic centre.

With economic globalization comes, of course, the relative and needs-based universalization of the political, technological, cultural, educational, and labour components of people's lives. Therefore, it goes without saying that with the mass movement of people across countries and continents already underway, the globalization of difference in cultures, languages, value systems, modes, and methods of economic and business management, levels of aspirations and possibilities of failure, and individual and community relationships as well as the programs of education that would permeate many of these, all carry with them notions and realities of difference that will be, *ipso facto*, globalized. Naturally and in the current state of world affairs, human beings would subordinate any visible and/or latent differences to the realities of economic advancement and to better livelihood possibilities for themselves. Moreover, those whose skills are needed elsewhere will most probably obey a cardinal principle of globalization, which stipulates (in effect, recommends) that they should arrive at where the lowest common denominator will be met. That is, in the now-too-familiar way of globalized and globalizing spaces, labour may choose to fly to the countries and regions where the best wages and conditions of employment are available. In Stromquist's terms:

> Globalization, with the creation of increasing economic power and employment opportunities in the North, has generated unprecedented physical mobility towards this area. Emigration from Sub-Saharan countries and Central European countries to Europe, and emigration from Latin America to the United States and Canada have undeniable impacts on educational systems in Northern countries. The impact is twofold, given the bipolar nature of immigration to these countries. On the one hand are the English-speaking children of sophisticated professionals who come here to work in cutting-edge firms as those in the electronics and bio-technical industries. On the other are the large masses of non-English speaking children of semi-literate and even illiterate parents (2002, pp. 2–3).

Here, it is clear that in the global movement of people and related issues, some will arrive less endowed than others, and will have a better opportunity to exploit available socio-economic and cultural possibilities in the new country. But an important point that must be advanced in these analyses is that previous hardships, once the individual or the group is in the new, more opportune, circumstances, should in no way diminish the possibilities that they could see and grasp to harness select advantages that could facilitate new and situationally reliable springboards, mostly through education, that could help them achieve better possibilities for themselves and for their children. Needless to add that an already available advantage in this regard is the initial determination of the groups, complemented by the policy-wise recommended readiness of Western educators and educational institutions to welcome and develop quasi-receptive structures that should deal effectively with the fact of globalized ethnic and racial differences and the educational demands they bring with them. Palmer and Hines' points in this regard are so cogent that it is worth quoting them at some length.

> As the dawn of the 21st Century slowly fades into the background, one aspect of the world seems apparent: we are living in an era of both expanding globalization and increasing ethnic and racial diversity in our local communities. Embedded within these demographic shifts is the need to challenge existing discriminatory policies, with the end hope of developing a national identity that encompasses people from all ethnic, racial and cultural backgrounds. Educational policy continues to be at the forefront in confronting institutional and social discrimination against minority and other oppressed groups. As a result, educational research provides fertile grounds where tensions between dominant groups and minority groups can be located and examined" (Palmer and Hines, 2002, p. 1).

It is also true that the new waves of immigrants, refugees, and so-called mobile professionals, mostly from the less developed Third World countries, will come to the West, and have already come with religio-cultural, educational and related value systems that may not only be different, but at times antithetical to those practiced by the dominant societies that manage both opportunities and public relationships in the former's new countries of residence. While the role of education in mediating differences has been promulgated in Canada and other Western countries with huge immigrant populations for some time, the possibilities for achieving a non-discriminatory identity has been, at best, limited. As such, the role of education in a country like Canada to effectively deal with so much globalized difference that touches the lives of almost all Canadians is as important as ever.

Moreover, the role of education in addressing and dealing with difference is heightened not only because others want to come to the West, but also because of falling birth rates in almost all Western countries, which, via the problematic of new demographic realities and its potentially adverse affects on the quality life, forces these countries to accept millions of new immigrants from other parts of the world. A good example in this case is Canada, where the 2001 census results indicate that in the coming five years, the country will be short one million skilled workers. With these realities, the current government is opening up to new possibilities in its immigration policy. This is partially triggered by the knowledge that continually falling birth rates are not likely to increase in the foreseeable future, and that the only way to deal with the situation is to increase the number of immigrants that are allowed to come to Canada every year to over 300,000. Issues of population growth and decline in this regard are more than just a desire for a given level of population. They directly, and at times urgently, affect services, health care quality and maintenance, as well as the required tax base to assure that Canadians continue enjoying the high standard of living they are used to. In addition, low or declining birth rates are complemented by an increasingly aging population, with the number of Canadian seniors expected to double from the present 4.2 million to 8.6 million within the next 20 years.

Again, with most immigrants coming from non-anglo, non-franco, and increasingly non-European sources (Scott, 2001; Ghosh, 1996), the role of education in constructively mediating the myriad of differences that the new immigrants, and more so their children, will bring to an already highly multicultural school and university setting will be paramount. As such, and depending on the care as well as the efficiency with which these programs are undertaken, they will either be conducive to the collective development of all Canadians, or to disjunctured and superficial discourses that are only multicultural in name (Abdi, 2002). The problem remains, however, at the societal and structural levels because government policies are slow to trickle down to government departments, and certainly to educational institutions, when they are accompanied by clear-cut and meaningful changes in practice.

The Post-September 11 World

"The great hope that a nation could wall itself off from the others is ... over" wrote Zygmunt Bauman (2002) about the United States after the events of September 11, 2001, more popularly known as 9-11. Perhaps one of the more profound effects of these tragic events has been the realization for people in the West, particularly Americans, that, "for better or worse [they] are a part of a globalized system, the effects of which cannot be completely controlled" (Giroux: 2002:1).

September 11 has become an important watershed in contemporary human history. And if there is anyone on planet earth who somehow missed the force of the event, it was on that fateful day when 19 hijackers, in the service of the now stupendously famous and previously Afghanistan-based Saudi millionaire and master terrorist Osama bin Laden, simultaneously slammed passenger airplanes into the World Trade Center towers in New York City and the United States Pentagon building in Washington, DC, killing thousands of people, and creating, in the process, a new level and space of the globalization of terrorism. This new perspective of terrorism has managed, with great efficiency, to hit the contemporary world's most powerful nation in the heart of its economic and military powers. As should have been expected, September 11 ignited the emotions of many Americans, especially in the critical first weeks of the attack, with fear, grief, media attention, and paranoia all combined to stir the patriotic emotions of Americans (Somers and Somers-Willett, 2002). September 11 has also deeply touched the psychological domain of the United States public where, in Michael Apple's terms:

> [Americans] had now become the world's oppressed. The (always relatively weak) recognition of the realities of the Palestinians, or the poor in what we arrogantly call "the third world" was now evacuated. Almost immediately, there were a multitude of instances throughout the nation of people who "looked Arabic" being threatened and harassed on the street, in schools, and in their places of business (2002, pp. 3–4).

Giroux (2002, p. 2) also points out how, "in the six weeks after 11 September, civil rights groups estimate that there were at least six murders and one thousand serious assaults committed against people perceived as 'Arab' or 'Muslim', including several hundred attacks on Sikhs." These were complemented by "the indefinite detention by federal authorities of over 11,000 immigrants, only four of whom have direct links to terrorist groups." The targeting of Sikhs, and the othering of people who appear Middle Eastern or South Asian, not only shows sheer ignorance on the part of some Americans who perpetuated crimes against innocent people, but also of airlines and other authorities such as immigration officers who continue to harass law-abiding people who, from a distance, fit *a priori* assumed racial and religious profiles.

To be fair, though, one must highlight, as Apple (2002) states—and this is definitely a welcome point in education's role in the globalization of difference even in the tough times of post September 11—the reality of the lesser-known instances of people's ethical complexities in supporting and meeting with Islamic students and others who may have felt threatened. These were positively enhanced by the critically situated understanding of many Americans that in order to guarantee rights and safety for all, the notion as well as the practice of the sanctity of all human lives must be universalized. Here, the point could be clarified: while September 11 was a tragedy that touched many lives, it might also present an opportunity to initiate a more all-world-centric consideration of how our lives are interconnected. With that, perhaps we should focus more on what we have in common by refraining from the—at times self-serving—campaigns of de-demo-nizing the other, the different, and the dangerously exotic, and seize, instead of running away from them, moments and momentous cases of difference that are fast becoming permanent features in our lives. A critical appreciation of this, which should give us a universal patri-otism, would, as Apple notes in his book, *Official Knowledge* (2000), procure, for most of us, a pragmatic and culturally inclusive return to a more humane [global] national space.

For educators at all levels, the events of September 11 offer both opportunities and dangers. On the one hand is the opportunity to develop in students a critical stance on history and understanding of people around the world, because these acts of terrorism cannot be understood without pointing to the connections between national and international contexts. Educators have the opportu-nity to "reclaim schools as democratic public spheres" (Giroux, 2003 p. 6) and to create spaces in classrooms to unveil the responsibili-ties of critical citizenship. On the other hand, the sudden outburst of intolerance in many countries of the West, particularly in the United States, where it was legitimized by legislation (the Patriot Act of 2002) makes it almost impossible for educators (in schools or universities) to deal with foreign policy issues critically. As George W. Bush has said, "if you are not with us you are against us." Several critical thinkers have pointed out that dissent is not unpatriotic, and have described the criticism and punishment for those who dared to voice dissent against policies such as racial profiling and the crim-inalization of social policies (Giroux, 2003). The very essence of democracy is in question because the concept of a just society is wavering: freedom, equity, and justice are changing concepts in today's world. Merely dissenting is not enough, because the result of these changing meanings will have far-reaching effects. Educators need to deconstruct the contradictory responses to the events of September 11, and to link that to globalization, to the domination of countries and of populations within countries, and to the culture of fear that has since developed.

The practical case of September 11, and the potential promise of humanity's positive possibilities aside, the United States, as expected, promised to retaliate, and it did, with a relentless aerial bombardment in southwestern Afghanistan that has led to the fall of the Taliban government, the death of thousands of Afghani soldiers and civilians, and the presumed fall of bin Laden's al-Qaida terrorist structure and organization. Here, Samuel Huntingon's much-maligned thesis on the clash of civilizations (see Huntington, 1993, 1996) was to be de-shelved by many analysts. That, even if one would want to believe that the global project of Osama bin Laden is not advancing civilization; rather, it is purely based on essentially isolationist religious fanaticism.

On the other hand, other people—and without minimizing the killing of so many innocent people in the World Trade Center—have died in different wars and in other unwarranted surprise attacks, not in the thousands, but perhaps in the hundreds of thousands. So why was this tragedy more important than the rest? Here the role of education and, more importantly, the media in globalizing difference, not in the sense we are using it in this work, but in the fact that one's position in the tragically misnamed global village (in this case the United States as the only superpower and by direct extension, Americans as the only first class citizens of the world) was pragmatically conspicuous in reminding us that, indeed, the death of Americans, especially at the hands of less endowed Middle Eastern fanatics, was a universal crime, and must be confronted with universal scorn and action. But there is at least one American academic who refuses to limit the planning as well as the implementation of terrorist acts to the (essentially mislabelled but still so-called) world of Islamic fundamentalists. This is, indeed, the case of the hard-hitting critic Noam Chomsky, who states in his aptly titled and popular book, *9-11* (2001), that terrorism is not a program solely operated by angry men from the fringes of the world, but has also been a practice utilized by, among others, the American government and its agents and institutions. Chomsky actually goes so far as to say that capitalist globalization was at least partially responsible for the September 11 attacks, and to support his point, chronicles what he terms as a series of terrorist acts and programs by successive American administrations. In a related but non-accusatory point, the Nobel Laureate Amartya Sen (2002) also instructs how Islam, comparatively speaking, never had a monopoly on religious intolerance or religious-based terrorism and killings. Sen adds that in many instances when religious persecution was in full force in Europe, Islamic emperors such as India's Akbar, the Great Mughul, were advancing, in fact practicing, the peaceful coexistence of all peoples and religions.

That being as it may, it was interesting that in the rush to assure America that all the good guys were on their side, initially by their immediate allies and later by almost every country in the world, the Canadian reaction, undoubtedly with a number of practical and analytical variations, may have essentially exposed the fundamental weaknesses that this northern country faces when the critical hour comes to deal with its powerful southern neighbour. While going into detail is not warranted in this context, it was noteworthy to see how the differences in this case were not only not highlighted, but were, at least from the perspective of the Canadian media, *ipso facto* erased. Here, the attack on Americans became an attack on "us." The question of the times, why they hate and want to kill

Americans, became why they hate "us" and want to kill "us." The habitual line of the American political and military establishment of how they should retaliate became how "we" should retaliate, and the now familiar American public parlance of protecting America, at all costs, from Islamic terrorism, literally became how "we" must keep these "terrorists" out of our lives. So much was this collusion of the emotional core of the two countries that one of the authors decided to ask students in a graduate seminar why the people of this country were so willingly and so suddenly doing this. Again, the sharing of grief with a country that is so economically, culturally, and linguistically close to the majority of Canadians was understandable, but many Canadians, in the pre-September 11 world, were also vociferous in assuring that they were, in so many accounts, different from the Americans. The responses from the students were mostly pragmatic, mainly repeating the primordial and modern linkages stated above. But perhaps there was more than that, including the generally latent but occasionally resurfacing threads of atavistic tribal attachments that, at least subliminally, affirm that when the critical hour comes, the enemies of those who share specific, concretizable traits with us are, without qualifications, also our permanent enemies.

Incidentally, Canadians, at least at the official political level, may not win the trophy for the most pro-American outburst in the post-September 11 world. The British political establishment, especially Prime Minister Tony Blair, has become so attached to the American anti-terrorism and war cause that some, including a good percentage of the British public, have questioned whether he has become more American than George W. Bush. Here again, the primordial attachments could not be discounted, but as in the Canadian case, some global psychosocial issues should have also been at stake. In the process, the long-ago globalized difference between the good and bad guys, with questions about any rapprochement absolutely not needed, were once again fortified in the post-September 11 world. But for educators who must develop alternative relationships with globalized difference, important questions relating to September 11 and beyond must be raised, and critically, not emotionally, answered. Especially important for global critical educators is how to uphold viable national citizenship education programs in order for students to be better informed when crises of this and similar natures come by. To effectively deal with these and related issues, and achieve a better national and global perspective, one would do well to heed Giroux's important observation that "Educators need to take a more critical position, arguing that critical knowledge, debate, and dialogue grounded in pressing social problems offers individuals and groups some hope in shaping the conditions that bear down on their lives .... [This would allow us all] to revitalize the language of civic education and democratization as part of a broader discourse of political agency and critical citizenship in a global world" (Giroux, 2002, p. 11).

It would also be necessary to elevate the level of debate, and take it to the new zones of legality and justice for workers, and especially academics, attacked and fired in the turbulent times of the post-September 11 world (Somers and Somers-Willett, 2002). Here, difference at the highest levels of academia, where critical thinking, cogent analysis and freedom of expression were supposed to be upheld, was sinisterly used to violate the rights of people whose patriotism was selectively questionable. As a result, the academic liberty of university professors, which stipulates full freedom in research and publication, in the classroom, and in issues related to extramural expressions (See Somers and Somers-Willett, 2002) was being increasingly put in jeopardy.

While "[o]ne hundred and fifty complaints of campus free speech violations were reported in the two months following September 11" (Somers and Somers-Willett, 2002, p. 6), the most prominent cases in this regard involved both institutional and popular attacks on

Sami Al-Arian, a professor of computer science at the University of South Florida, and Robert Jensen, a professor of journalism at the University of Texas at Austin. Al-Arian has since been jailed for allegedly supporting terrorism many years before 9/11. In Canada, something akin to this might have happened when members of parliament from the opposition populist party, the Canadian Alliance (now the Conservative Party of Canada), called for an official government response to some lines in a new book entitled *On Equilibrium* (2001) by the prominent Canadian writer and social critic, John Ralston Saul. Saul pointed out how demonizing Islam will not solve the problem, adding that in the "sweep of history, Christian militancy has wreaked far greater destruction than anything managed by Islam" (p. 87).

Again, the number, as well as the socio-political intensity, of those voices that managed to warn about the extraneous introduction of collective punishment, in the midst of post-September 11 fervent patriotism, into a fundamentally individual rights-oriented American (Western) democracy, while few and scattered, were still being heard. In commenting on how educators should respond to the situation, the critical pedagogue Henry Giroux writes,

> [It is important that educators] use their classrooms not only to help students to think critically about the world around them but also to offer a sanctuary and forum where they can address their fears, anger, and concerns about the events of September 11 and how it has affected their lives. The events of September 11 provide educators with a crucial opportunity to reclaim schools as democratic public spheres in which students can engage in dialogue and critique around the meaning of democratic values, the relationship between learning and civic engagement, and the connection between schooling, what it means to be a critical citizen, and the responsibilities one has to the larger world (2002, pp. 3–4).

Again, the potential return of the McCarthy-esque world (Somers and Somers-Willett, 2002) was, to say the least, frightening. One must assume, though, that with a desirable dose of positive thinking, the fundamental tenets of both American and Canadian democracies have been tested many times, and even if there were some unwarranted but essentially self-inflicted failures such as McCarthyism and the incarceration of, for example, people of Japanese extraction in both countries in World War II, these may now be at a point where basic rights for citizens, residents, and others are safeguarded. As some of us should know, though, foreigners, especially in the United States where so many lives were lost to the September 11 attacks, could be on their own in the most powerful democracy in the world. Here again, the role of educators as democratic workers cannot be overestimated. As Giroux centrally notes in his book, *Public Spaces, Private Lives* (2001), the ongoing project of critical pedagogy may be our best hope for achieving an expansive possibility of social transformation that should, at least partially, affirm a universal commitment to the needs as well as the aspirations of all.

Education and the Positive Globalization of Difference

Whether it is weaving through the myriad themes and practices of globalization, analytically and policy-wise complemented by special regional or worldwide crises such as the one induced by the September 11 terrorist attack, dealing with difference is no longer an option. It is, *prima facie*, central to all the possibilities that learning programs must address in this widely expanding and, at the same time, perceptibly shrinking world. While people who are different from the European norm already form multicultural societies, it must be emphasized that globalization today has made large movements of people an expected phenomenon, so new arrivals come to a society that does not treat them the same way as their predecessors who were expected to become invisible (while they were targeted for being physically visible). However, the recognition of difference and the implementation of educational programs undertaken through a political culture of acceptance and understanding is not, and should not be, exclusively the work of host countries and their people. It is also imperative that new immigrants prepare themselves to do their part in constructively explaining their experiences and traditional worldviews to the new spaces where they intend to reside in and establish new lives. But they must be given the space to express themselves. In addition, new Canadians would, for example, seek and highlight points of cultural, educational, and aspirational compatibilities with their new compatriots, and would strive to philosophically lessen select corners of potential friction that could anatagonize others, and could in the process at best slow their mobility in achieving what instigated their transmigration in the first place: lack of desired opportunities, or even viable livelihood possibilities, in their original countries, and a new determination to go to a new place and accomplish specific goals and objectives.

This does not mean at all, at least in the Canadian context, that people will shed their primordial cultural and ontological packages and become Canadians overnight. While the conditions in the new country should not discourage, and may facilitate, the continuity of the home cultures, languages, and previously acquired, specialized mechanisms of life management, the emphasis should be on the opportunities and equal chances afforded to the new arrivals in the new country. What this essentially means is that in order to achieve as many of one's objectives as possible, one must seek out, and even intentionally attempt to influence, zones of educational and employment comfort that could be expanded to sustainably benefit both communities. These zones of social cohesion could be transformed into culturally welcoming possibilities that would also adhere to the principles of efficiency that may be necessary in order for the new immigrant to maximize both the longitudinal and latitudinal dimensions of the new chances, which might allow him or her to successfully compete with those who have had the added advantage of being native to the culture as well as the language in which the opportunity, in both its descriptive and operational modes, was created in the first place.

Here, and while one is advised to take it with a grain of salt, the provisional attributes of the cultural third space (see Bhabha, 1994) might lessen the possible frictions that the two social sub-sets that are—both voluntarily and involuntarily—coming together, would bring with them. After all, it may not be surprising to be curious about people and situations that one is not familiar with. But again, as Matustik (1998) points out, the trouble with the otherwise benign third space is that it could instigate the quasi-unavoidable clash of cultural possibilities that are not equally endowed in their power codifications, with the almost assured reality that the dominant culture would continually subordinate the other. That being as it may, it is also true that the two cultures that have been previously separated, to use a Renanian expression (see Renan, 1990), by seas, rivers, and mountains, are now sharing one national enterprise, and as such have to come together. In addition, while radical equality is generally an ideal, some situations are more conducive to the manageable coexistence of different cultures, and among the countries of the world, Canada could qualify as one such place.

To explicate the importance of new immigrants not always waiting for help from others in the new country, but becoming the vanguard of their empowerment, one could selectively borrow the Gramscian notion of people systematically understanding the social and cultural situations where they could be disadvantaged. To overcome that, the disadvantaged would acquire the necessary intellectual and pragmatic understanding, and equip themselves with the necessary tools to move to the mainstream of the political and economic life in the new social power formations (Mayo, 1999). In the context of globalized difference, the have-nots (new immigrants) would do well if they, together with the established groups, see the important premium that should be placed on the potentially emerging hybridized cultures that could bring about and sustain new collective horizons and converging cultural and difference sub-sets that would enrich the lives of all.

It is true that globalization, in both its conceptual implications and pragmatic possibilities, aims for the homogenization of people's worldview, consumer needs and even socio-economic relationships. While that is a fact of globalization, it would be incumbent upon teachers that instead of suppressing differences, these should be appreciated, and educational programs should aim for the sharing of the richness that results from the diverse cultural sub-sets that will continue coming together in such multi-ethnic countries as Canada, the United Kingdom, and the United States. It is also important to realize that ascertaining and appreciating the constructive sides of difference, beyond the simplistic accommodation or the selectively ephemeral tolerance of other people and backgrounds, must be paramount in all educational programs that claim any sense of multiculturalism in their agenda. Genuine multicultural education that welcomes the fact of globalized difference must lead to the unconditional and permanent acceptance of differences that should, via all possible legitimate means, be given a safe space in the multi-ethnic national project.

The point here is that there is a direct relationship between the positive and accepted globalization of difference, and the upholding of fundamental human rights and freedoms that are at crossroads in all of the world's rapidly globalizing spaces. Again, while education is generally seen as enhancing democratic rights and responsibilities (Enslin, 1999; Tilak, 1994; Dewey, 1926) as well as elevated notions of universal freedoms and awareness, it is also the case that in the recent history of humanity, those who claimed higher stages of education and overall enlightenment were, more than otherwise, responsible for some of the worst human rights violations. As such, the interesting twist in this regard is that those who formulated and implemented such global crimes as slavery, the importation of millions of indentured labourers, colonialism, and subsequent genocidal and ethnic cleansing projects, were all claiming that they were in a higher state of civilizational achievement than their victims. Colonialism has been, for example, portrayed by Europeans as an important civilizing mission that was to cleanse the coloured continents of the world of barbarism. But the civilizing mission, was, *ipso facto*, responsible for the optimum and premeditated destruction of people, lands, cultures and perhaps, above all else, the psychological being of the colonized (Nandy, 1997; Memmi, 1991; Fanon, 1968, 1967). Here, the role of educators would go beyond the righting of possible contemporary wrongs, and strive for the reintroducing—not for the perpetuation of victimhood but as important historical lessons that we should all learn from—of past human rights violations coupled with the validation of different forms of resistance that people have used to liberate themselves from oppression.

The collective understanding that results from these important exercises should be used as a conveyor to move to the current multicultural spaces where difference, in all its forms and facets, should never be used to justify new violations of people's freedom. As such, the right to education that will be harnessed by new groups that are coming to new countries must be intermeshed with practices assuring that such education speaks for and represents all humanity including the still valid Deweyian (Dewey, 1952) and current multicultural education notion (Giroux, 2000; McLaren, 1997; Nieto, 1992) that learners must see not only their stake, but also and equally important, their background, in the type of education they are receiving. This, indeed, is the core of any critical pedagogy that selectively aims not only for the full inclusion of all interests and needs, but for the radical equalization of possibilities that could be harvested by different actors from a given educational enterprise. In such cases, one possible educational response to the globalization of difference is to highlight the positive strength of that difference to optimize the power of collective human agency. Here, one should agree with Martha Nussbaum (1998), that in the difference-bound spaces of the globe, we must embrace new versions of multicultur-alizing liberal education so as to achieve the coming about of criti-cal thinkers who work for world citizenship. As such, Snauwaert (2001, p. 4) should be speaking for the majority of the world's citi-zens when he writes that "our shared humanity carries with it a moral imperative to respect the dignity of every human life ... [this belief is] grounded in the customs and principles of democratic societies and the international community." Implicit in this collec-tive human project is the project of constructive resistance by those who may otherwise be marginalized simply because they are differ-ent, to yield to any practically or existentially alienating enterprise, and always believe, as Alain Badiou (cited in Giroux, 2002, p. 12) notes, that "the space of the possible is larger than the one assigned—that something else is possible, but not that everything is possible."

As important as the objectives and contents of conventional educational programs in terms of accepting and exploiting the good points of difference are the quality of learning and other related messages conveyed via the relatively new media of the internet. And while educational technology has had a good number of positive effects, and the efficiency as well as the rapid transfer of messages, information, and research can only be appreciated, it is also the case that those who spread hate and difference-based discrimination against minorities in Western countries have found the World Wide Web an excellent and highly effective tool with which to preach their hatred and expand the message of their racist ideology to every corner of the earth. Among the most important, and at times captive, audience of these hate groups are school-age children and early-years university students, who may be taken in by the falsely concocted emotional stirrings with which established bigots are relentlessly bombarding them. As Stromquist (2002, p. 3) tells us, the information technology and communications media exert powerful influences that are many times more than the effects of schooling on children and young teenagers. While we would do well to trust the capacity of these young people to critically evaluate the messages they are receiving, it will always be the case that some of the messages will get through, and some youngsters and older folks will see cultural and other differences as problems that should be attacked along with people from minority groups, because they are perceived to embody these differences, hence becoming targets.

An important educational objective must therefore become, especially in places like Canada and other multicultural societies, the creation as well as the sustainability of new reliable means to counterweigh, as much as possible, the destructive and deplorable schemes of racist bigots. In their minds, these people have concluded that a psychological or physical attack on difference will alleviate their own shortcomings, and allow them to claim some kind of achievement in societies where an overwhelming majority of them are perennial underachievers. In all, an important aspect of the globalized difference must be the exposition as well as the prevention of human rights violations, especially those relying upon cultural, linguistic, or religious variations to claim their victims. To achieve that across the globe, the role of education and educators is crucial. After all, educators will, via their overt or even covert psychosocial dispositions, have a lasting, and many times a potentially impactful, influence over many of their students.

As such, and beyond classroom interactions, it will also be indispensable to include, at the policy level, crucial learning and coun-selling components that appreciate the importance of accepting difference as something that is good for society. These points must also be ingrained in all teacher training programs, including those that focus on, and are conveyed via, the internet and other instruc-tional technology. Teachers must also realize that beyond skills and moral training of students, they must also educate for globally situ-ated socio-political formations and as such must "continue finding ways of entering the world of politics by both making social problems visible and contesting their manifestation in the polity" (Giroux, 2002, p. 11). It is the case that in the post-Cold War world, and with the way that global commerce, cultural, and educational movements as well as labour and related issues are being globalized around the world, the reality of the global, cosmopolitan citizen is uncompromisingly emerging. Therefore, while education cannot serve as a ready panacea that solves all the livelihood hindrances that people's differences might aggravate, it will, nevertheless, remain an important and primary forum that facilitates the critical and positive understanding of people's differences as something that could be good for inter-personal and international understanding, and would make our world a better place in which to live.

CONCLUSION

The fact of globalization—in its economic, political, cultural, tech-nological as well as related and intervening educational and over-all difference dimensions and implications—is a fully accepted worldwide reality. Always central to the promises as well as the potential problems of globalization are the movement of people who, via the pragmatics of their desire and select willingness, are determined to seek better opportunities in places other than their areas of origin, and who are, in the process, shifting the demographics of their countries of destination, which are mostly the now post-industrial, information technology-driven countries of Western Europe and North America. The major trigger currently persuading immigrants, refugees, and select components of the so-called mobile professionals to move to the West is the availability of better opportunities in employment and education, especially for the children of migrants.

From the perspective of educators, these trends of globalization also involve the massive globalization of difference. From now and into the foreseeable future, humanity's flow across borders, especially a sizable chunk of the world's disenfranchised hundreds of millions, will come with numerous and different cultural, linguistic, and other learning and teaching needs and challenges in the new countries of residency. The new groups, even if they are from the same national space, will not be homogenous in their educational needs and capacities. Some of them would be well-educated but in a different context, some less educated, and still others, especially children with refugee families from refugee camps in Africa, Asia, and Latin America, hardly educated or not educated at all. Here, the required critical learning and teaching services rendered by educators and educational institutions must be parallel with the pragmatic notions of multiculturalism and practical multicultural pedagogy that do not simply tolerate the exponentially rising facts of difference, but will uncompromisingly respect and accept the myriad of positive possibilities that could be harnessed and reconstructed from the previously disjunctured cultural and linguistic spaces and relationships.

Moreover, especially after the tragic events of September 11, educators must incorporate new discussions and practicalities of citizenship education that fully respect the rights of all into their programs and spheres of teaching, paving the way for the formation of new cosmopolitan citizens whose international understanding and sensitivities are globally located and oriented. In sum, we must, as the responsible teachers of students from all corners of the world, strive for the intellectual and moral development of globally conscious learners. As mature citizens of their countries in the near future, these learners would prioritize the praxis of the horizontally expansive good that could come from comprehensively developed and critically nurtured public spaces that are culturally inclusive and, without contravening currents, difference-friendly.

5 | MULTICULTURAL EDUCATION IN THE FUTURE

Whatever you can do or dream you can, begin it. Boldness has genius, power and magic in it.

—Goethe

What are the educational implications of the paradigm shift? The new paradigm has several characteristics. It is a new worldview, which is emerging in several areas in society and the academic disciplines: the humanities, social, and natural sciences. In academia, it is already selectively shaking the traditional foundations of knowledge, and proposes to transpose the meaning and function of education at all levels. The new worldview is rooted in a perception of reality that makes knowledge multicultural, global, and interdependent. It makes the educational act political, moral, and intellectual. It shifts the focus in education from content and technology to a process that is democratic, dialogical, and humane. The following then are the main ideas of a new worldview in education. They are also the ones for a reconceptualized multicultural education, for good education is inclusive: it represents the whole. The first three ideas refer to the relationship of education and society; the next three describe education as a process; and the final point is an examination of education's role in the future.

First of all, education is the understanding of the unity and mutual inter-relationship of all experiences and phenomena. In teaching to experience the world, the education process recognizes the dynamics of the whole. It emphasizes the fundamental interdependence of all phenomena by developing an ecological awareness. This means that education must have a global perspective, and an affinity with humanity within and beyond national boundaries. It also means that students must learn to analyze the different conditions of people in their own societies and across the world. The idea of the basic oneness of all phenomena is the very essence of Eastern philosophies. Capra (1991) explains that ordinarily we divide the world into separate objects—us and them—because we are not aware of a basic unity. While this division may be useful in helping us cope, it is not a fundamental feature of reality. In Hinduism and Buddhism, for example, the idea of dividing the world into separate entities is a product of the mind, an illusion based on ignorance. The differences and contrasts we create are relative within an all-embracing unity. That is because opposites are created relationally: "When all in the world know the beautiful as beauty/ There appears ugliness/ When they know goodness as good/ There appears evil" (Lao Zi, Chapter II).

Opposites are merely two sides of the same coin. The notion of dynamic balance and interplay is important. The Chinese symbolize the yin (female) and yang (male) as being in a dynamic unity. The fundamental idea in Eastern thought is to move beyond the world of intellectual distinctions to a spiritual world of non-distinction. Feminist and postmodernist theories have focused on the social construction of difference, and challenge the legitimacy built for one over the other: male over female, white over black, middle class over working class. Multicultural education is an attempt at a dynamic unity of socially constructed opposites and differences. The good/bad opposition is a devaluation. It is the naming of an inferiority in relation to a superior standard of humanity. The categorical opposition of groups objectifies and represses the differences within the groups. In this way the definition of difference as exclusion and opposition actually denies difference. The essence of multiculturalism is a culture of commonality across differences. It is unity within diversity: a recognition of differences and collectivity. Implicit in this concept is the dynamic possibility of heterogeneity as an instrument for realizing democratic unity. We cannot be different on our own. Multiculturalism is about creating new spaces, creating a we, by bringing together people across borders. As Courts (1997, p. 25) notes, "as educators, we need to encourage and sustain difference, when possible, without encouraging or creating enemies."

The problem in education is the representation of the norm in the image of the elite. A patriarchal Eurocentric curriculum imposes the image of the colonizer (the dominant group) as the norm. The other is devalued as well as depreciated in being evaluated against that norm. The inclusion of other worldviews in the curriculum is necessary in order to change the negative self-image of the other, to shape an identity that is not distorted by exclusion. Judgments regarding which knowledge is of the greatest worth can hardly be made on partial knowledge, because prejudice and denial of equal status are implicit in such an approach.

Furthermore, judging different ways of doing things from one point of view is also biased. The yardsticks for judgment will need transformation. This is only possible in a syncretic development, by creating a new space, and by the "fusion of horizons" (Taylor, 1994). It is through such fusion that we are able to develop new vocabularies of comparison. The willingness to study other worldviews will necessarily displace the centre. But the aim of a redefined multicultural education is that ultimately there should be no centre, no periphery. The problem with the unity aspect of multiculturalism has been that assimilation, and even integration, of minority groups does not imply equal effort. The dominant group is not required to make any overtures towards integration. The survival of minority groups, however, demands that they learn the majority culture and language. This asymmetrical phenomenon undermines the meaning of multiculturalism. The asymmetry may also imply that multicultural education is, and may remain, a major terrain of struggle where progressive, democratic forces face those who are bent on preserving the status quo (Carlson, 1997). To achieve that, we must, as educators and others, succeed in highlighting the important notion that the politics of recognition underlying multiculturalism is not only an affirmation of difference, but a recognition of the interconnectedness of various ethnocultural groups: of men and women working together, sharing the world, and caring about each other. For example, "one of the most difficult problems in critical feminist theory today is conceptualizing the interconnections of race, class and gender" (Muszyski, 1991, p. 64). Adrienne Rich (1986) referred to this as the politics of location, because power depends upon one's location in various sites such as gender, class, race, and ethnicity. The social construction of knowledge as well as a changing historical reality are a challenge to the West to re-examine the equation with "other cultures, other states, other histories, other experiences, traditions, peoples, and destinies" (Said, 1989, p. 216).

Secondly, multicultural education is built on the recognition of the democratic principles of universal dignity, equality (actually equity), and fairness. As Giroux (2001, 2002) so emphatically proposes, in any society that claims to be democratic, regardless of the type of political system or processes to achieve a responsive and responsible public office, education must equip all children and adults with the forum and the necessary concomitant empowering schemes to be equal relative to all national institutions and spaces. Democracy is misinterpreted in liberal versions of multiculturalism because the politics of equal dignity are translated as being blind (supposedly neutral) to differences, which, in undetectable and unconscious ways, promote established discriminatory regimes that, for lack of a better expression, rigidify the perennially eschewed status. Equal recognition of the dignity of human beings despite differences, as stated in human rights charters, is an essential component of democratic culture, and implies equal status of different cultures and people irrespective of sex, race, ethnicity, religion, etc. This is the interpretation of democracy in the redefined multicultural education.

The liberal multicultural position in effect endorses inequality by emphasizing that people differ, but that equality is possible if sameness is achieved. In other words, as a liberal concept, equality negates identity and is parallel to sameness. The redefined multicultural view, however, challenges the idea of equality as equivalent to sameness. The liberal view of equal dignity is blind to difference as an essential component of democracy. The liberal view is an assault on the notion of distinctiveness, and this suppression of identity becomes problematic and potentially inhuman. The assumption of a universal, difference-blind principle constructs the North American middle class male as the ideal. It is not possible (nor desirable) to wish human differences away.

In education, colour-blind policies and striving for sameness despite gender, race, ethnicity, and class differences becomes paternalistic, perpetuating hierarchy through the appearance of equality in the educational system. Charles Taylor points out that blind liberalisms themselves reflect particular cultures, "particularism masquerading as the universal" (Taylor, 1994, p. 85). The change in the new worldview is to shift the focus away from sameness to difference. It is transformative and radical, and therefore a paradigm shift. This is a new politics, the politics of difference, the demand for recognition as different but of equal worth by females and ethnocultural groups. This recognition is linked to identity, the defining of characteristics as to who we are as human beings. The irony is that because people have been thought to be different, they have faced discrimination. This very identity, when given negative characteristics, results in imprisoning someone in a false, generally distorted, and existentially diminished mode of existence. Not only does this discrimination mean a lack of due respect, but it can directly harm people. As such, unconditional recognition becomes a primary need of human beings. So it is not simply the recognition of difference, but equality with differences that is the salient point. Expressed differently, skin colour, race, ethnicity, sex, and class are irrelevant characteristics in measuring equality, as the provisions in equal rights charters confirm.

Discrimination based on prejudice and bias always implies a denial of universal dignity. It is a major assault on human dignity. Non-discrimination involves being colour sensitive and being aware of differences rather than concealing them. It affirms that differences are recognized as the basis for which equality of treatment can be given. This sometimes may imply not the same treatment, but fair treatment, which may even mean differential treatment. Equity policies come under this practice. It is important to remember that such temporary measures for those who have been historically disadvantaged are aimed at a future when the playing field will be level and equity policies will no longer be necessary. Omission of the history, culture, and experiences of non-Europeans, females, and working class people in the school curriculum is a denial of the fundamental principle of human dignity. Moreover, the curriculum is biased because the knowledge is partial, and it is also insensitive and boring, with its narrow and unitary perspective.

In classroom interaction, the denial of the principle of universal dignity is subtle and often invisible. Research indicates that physical and cultural differences do make a difference, not biologically, but because people have different experiences and worldviews. Differences, as Gaskell (1989, p. 49) previously reminded us, exist as "to how people live, what toys they play with as children, who their friends are, how much power they are able to exercise in the world, and how others talk to them." These differences imply a variation in the ways diverse children learn best, and the best way to determine which one will work best should be reached via discussions that are openly and constructively undertaken to give the best possible education to all children. Students are not getting an equal education if that education is based on a model of development of one group that apparently cannot help but value dominant modes of elevating rationalism and objectivity over other ways knowing and valuating.

The effects of race on victims are hurtful, and make their school experiences sad, firstly through subjective means such as loss of self-esteem, conflicts and vulnerability, and secondly through objective means such as unequal opportunity in school, resulting in poor performance and ultimately inequity in career, life choices, economic, and political power. Racism and discrimination do not only affect the victim. The belief in racism and its possible practice would also have a cluster of negative effects on those who are from the dominant segments of society, as they experience moral confusion and the development of a dual consciousness via their learning of hate, fear, and intolerance while, at the same time, being told of democratic values of equality and justice in relation to other people. These children could also develop distorted ideas of self in relation to those who are different, and construct meanings of difference that are incompatible with the ideals of democracy and a global society. An ethnocentric worldview deprives dominant group children of knowledge that would be enriching.

One way to affirm the dignity of students is to see different voices and perspectives as representing diverse opinions about the world that are enriching one another and, in the process, creating more inclusive and, in the long-run, socially more productive possibilities to all participants as well as to others who may come in contact with them. Any program or practice of education that silences pupils or people's voices is bound to diminish the inter-personal, even inter-generational, and international and global dialogue that would connect people, thus literally goes against the spirit as well as the realities of today's widely opening world forum. As such, if empowerment, across different relationships and spaces, is the aim of multicultural education, then learning that gives voice and a sense of personal control to every child must not only be the highest priority, but all aspects of education must be judged by the school's ability to be democratic towards all students.

Thirdly, epistemology is an integral part of education. Epistemology, contextually the understanding of the process of knowledge creation and learning in perceiving reality, challenges the idea of knowledge as object and objective. An epistemic view of knowledge, therefore, questions the metanarratives and universalizing tendency in the Eurocentric, male-stream worldview that is still being transmitted in many zones of the North American schooling system as the only reality. This rejection is based on an understanding of a world of multiple centres and possibilities where the radical equalization of all representations is uncompromisingly promoted and, at least, discursively achieved (Stam and Shohat, 1994). The rejection of a universalizing tendency has implications for definitions of excellence and success, evaluation and quantification of knowledge. The revolutionary shift in the understanding that knowledge is neither value-free nor context-free also means that pedagogy must take into account the real life experiences of the students, because the content and organization of knowledge is conditioned by the context and location of the knower.

Fourthly, education is a political process. The focus must move away from the content and mechanics of pedagogy to the politics of how power operates to create difference and maintain it. Teachers need more than technological knowledge. Teaching is related to reproduction, but needs to be linked to production as well. The process of education forms identities and self-concept—positive in some and negative in others. It empowers some through affirmation, disempowers others through experiences of racism and sexism, or both. Education must not only root students in history and culture, but also provide the conditions in which to develop a strong sense of citizenship. It must make students counterintuitive (Ng, 1993), that is, urge them to interrogate the natural ways of doing things in order to unveil domination and discrimination.

Dangerous conflicts around the globe, the effects of human insensitivity to, and brutality upon, other humans are a stern warning that schools can no longer avoid dealing with the root and cultural causes of domination, poverty, and unequal power relations. Education offers the possibility for a transformation in the relations of domination between men and women, and a redistribution of political and economic power between classes and races.

Fifthly, education is a moral endeavour. It involves developing an internal sense of self, and that is why the moral aspect of schooling is significant. It is the search for truth and meaning in the surrounding reality. But all knowledge is tentative, and even some scientific theories and observations are approximate rather than definitive. That is why the foundations of knowledge are shifting, and the concept of knowledge involves interactions that are extended through networks such as the information highway. The goals of education are generated by the moral commitment of society. The goals of the ends of life, about what the good life ought to be, are substantive goals. How life should be lived, in the pursuit of justice, fairness and equality, are procedural goals. The concept of justice involves education in moral values, whereas fairness and equality involve democratic values.

Sixthly, education is dialogical. Education emerges out of a dialectical interaction and interdependence. It is in the complexity of interactions that identities are produced. A multicultural education does not privilege any group or person, because differences are not taken to be a reason for exploitation. The paradox about individualized identity (monological) is that while we need it to define ourselves, it is fulfilled by our relationship with others (dialogical). But identity, even as definition of self, is constructed by where we come from, and involves the significant others (dialogical) who help us form this sense of self in the individual and cultural sense. We become fully human when we are capable of expression through language, art, culture, caring, and so on. The capacity to express is obtained through dialogical encounters, through interactions (Taylor, 1994). The capacity to express is a means to power, and language is an example of how power has been entrenched. The need for instruction in inclusive language not only means going beyond a simple prescription for new conventions, but to understand how our world and words are shaped by patriarchy. Non-sexist, non-racist language simply recognizes the principle of universal dignity.

The development of identity is negotiated daily through the school curriculum, and interactions and inter-relationships in the school culture. The fact that identity is also negotiated through dialogue with others, particularly significant others such as teachers and peer groups, makes the power equation in relations crucial. In that sense, interpersonal and social relations are the key *loci* of self-discovery and self-affirmation. Emotional expressions are significant because they are essential demonstrations of our inner self. That is why emotional development is also an essential part of the redefined multicultural education.

Finally, one hope for peace and survival of humanity in the face of war and environmental disasters lies in a radical transformation in the values and processes underlying education. The hope is in a critical democracy, not the kind of contemporary democracy where more people die in the streets than in wars. The kind of world we will have in this twenty-first century will depend upon the next generation. This implies an urgent need for a transformation in our schools and universities, which will mould the next generation. In short, what is really required is a compelling change of values, a change of heart. "How will the drama of democracy be played out in the twenty-first century?" asks Elshtain. "Are we citizens of Western democracies, in fact, in the danger zone?" (1993, pp. 3, 4). The democratic possibilities in the politics of difference and recognition are thwarted by the politics of displacement in which the "I" and the "we" cannot merge into a common space as distinct and be in harmony with each other. The category of citizen has become a matter of indifference, and one may rightly be disturbed by the loss of civil society. Yet, democracy is more than a set of principles, and involves the daily actions, the spirit and energy of a people. They must first know the "I" in order to be able to retain the "I" in creating a "we," in a fusion of horizons. The challenge of education is to define identity, knowledge, and cultural metaphors in shaping the lived experiences of students and provide meaning in democracy. For cultural minorities and women it may mean redefining identities within their multiple realities in relation to the politics of difference.

Iris Marion Young (1990) pointed to the need for redefining the meaning of social justice from the distribution of benefits and burdens among society's members, which emphasizes the consumer aspect of persons, to concepts of domination and oppression in a context that includes action, decisions, and developing capacities. Education has a significant role to play in this wider concept of social justice. This can be achieved through explaining the power relations, and examining the historical and social roots of persistent inequalities that democracy cannot endure for too long. The survival of the democratic experiment depends then on critical, thinking citizens. Educators must focus on the critical citizen: one who is directed by a set of values that embrace principles of universal dignity, democratic rights, and obligations. This would be part of the wider discourse on the politics of difference, which acknowledges changing identities, agency, and voice.

Educators must redefine society's view of what is excellent, worthy, and necessary. They must also recognize the need for economic skills, for without them democratic citizenship and political stability would be jeopardized. Education generally effects, for those who receive it, relatively higher levels of economic achievement, and if one important function of schooling is to prepare people for jobs with generally a direct relationship between a person's type of employment and his or her social status, then we should assume that education is perpetually linked to power. And to extend the possibly rewarding elasticity of the point, if conventional programs of education technically empowered those who were benefiting from the status quo, new possibilities of inclusive and multicultural schooling in the Canadian context and elsewhere must incorporate into their loop of empowerment all those who have been previously marginalized.

CONCLUSION

Education must be based on a commitment to the ideas of possibility and diversity. The assumptions underlying multicultural education are idealistic. But world events, including the September 11 tragedy in the United States (see Chapter IV), ensure that happenstances that could lead radical transformations in all aspects of our lives do take place. While we should expect that much good will and peaceful global understanding could prevail in our world, we also need to design our educational programs as both ideological and concrete possibilities that could counter-balance programs of hate, discord, and wanton destruction that may be, due to the fundamental makeup of human beings, a part of life on earth for the foreseeable future.

It is also true that how far society and school can accommodate the needs of all students depends on political will. The extent to which different value positions are incorporated in all aspects of societal and school life (structural pluralism) will be determined by the force of democracy. Difference can no longer be tolerated passively (passive cultural pluralism). It must be more than an explicit recognition of difference as the basis for allocation of resources and power (corporate cultural pluralism). Change must be structural, but it must also be a moral commitment to universal dignity. Schools, administrators, teachers, students, and parents at all levels will need to find new and better ways of preparing for a hope-filled future where the hearts of young people will join their minds to determine the fate of a shared tomorrow. The balance between personal, social, and political identities becomes central for pedagogy and teacher education.

The realities of immigration and the decline in the birthrate of Western nations pave the way for a fundamental change in the composition of school populations. In addition, given the fact that in some urban centres, minority students taken together form the numerical majority, the educational needs of those once assumed to be different can no longer be ignored. The response of the Canadian educational systems to the increasing diversity of the student population has generally been unimpressive and uneven, although Ontario stands out in its progressive efforts. The absence of a federal department of education is particularly evident in the lack of a multicultural education policy. This is essential for all students in all parts of the country because they cannot remain isolated from national and global, heterogeneous, and interdependent societies.

Any radically equiticizing notions and practices of multicultural education must begin with a vision of what education might be but is not. It is a commitment to democracy, to life. The vision itself must continue to grow. The issues explored in these pages provide a conceptual framework that recognizes our abilities to connect in creating a more humane social order. While education resists change, it is still the most significant vehicle for developing the concepts contained in the philosophy of multiculturalism. Education can make problems visible so that race, gender, class, and other inequities are not frozen in time, space, and history. Nor should the learning process be juxtaposed with a universalized norm within a framework defined by the privileged.

The rise in consciousness is evident in matters of gender equality. Statistics show that the problem of inequality remains, not only in racial/ethnic and class terms, but also in gender identities. The debate is currently intense and complex, and this gives reason for hope. Structural changes, which involve a new worldview, will be the hardest to bring about because they cause power imbalances. Equity legislation is slow to filter into schools. Not only does change involve policy issues, but also the daily experiences and practices where power imbalances are acted out. Refusing recognition to people is a form of oppression. It must be confronted and challenged by students, teachers, and administrators, as well as parents if they are all to be partners in education. What we teach the next generation is central to multicultural education.

The issue of emancipatory leadership is the focus of a new interest in education. The real challenge of leadership is to develop a critical imagination of how to create political and moral consciousness in all students as future citizens of a country and the globe for leading a humane life. This means broadening the definition of school and its goals to encompass difference as a basis for achieving a delicate balance between diversity and unity. It further means defining the purpose of schooling as providing a fair chance at success, not an equal opportunity for failure; to maximize the potential of all, not to separate the successful from the unsuccessful. The success of school depends not merely on test scores but also on the answer to the question: what kind of citizen is being produced? Ultimately, it is the child who is at the centre of the education process. Each child is unique, with a natural instinct to explore and to learn, with every new opportunity representing potential new excitement, happiness, and unique possibilities of achievement. The greatest injustice is to suppress a child's need to question, to dream, and to expect a viable and just stake in the school, neighbourhood, or national enterprise. In Paulo Freire's powerful words, learners, all learners, must prepare for the harnessing of tomorrow as a possible project. One of the most effective platforms to achieve this tomorrow, we suggest, is critically located multicultural education that, via inclusively polycentric praxis, speaks for, about, and to all students and by design and default, to their diverse world.

REFERENCES

Abdi, Ali (2001a). Integrated Education and Black Development in Post-Apartheid South Africa. *Compare: A Journal of Comparative Education* 31(2), 229–244.

Abdi, Ali (2001b). Identity in the Philosophies of Dewey and Freire: Select Analyses. *Journal of Educational Thought* 35(2), 181–200.

Abdi, Ali (2002). *Culture, Education and Development in South Africa: Historical and Contemporary Perspectives.* Westport and London: Bergin and Garvey.

Aboud, Frances (1993). The Developmental Psychology of Racial Prejudice. *Transcultural Psychiatric Research Review* 3, 229–242.

Achebe, Chinua (2000). *Home and Exile.* Oxford, UK: Oxford University Press.

Anderson, Alan and Frideres, James (1981). *Ethnicity in Canada: Theoretical Perspectives.* Toronto, ON: Butterworths.

Apple, Michael (1992). The Text and Cultural Politics. *Educational Researcher* 21(7), 4–11, 19.

Apple, Michael (1999). *Power, Meaning and Identity: Essays in Critical Educational Studies.* New York, NY: Peter Lang.

Apple, Michael (2000). *Official Knowledge* (2nd edn). New York, NY: Routledge.

Apple, Michael (2002). Patriotism, Pedagogy and Freedom: On the Educational Meanings of September 11. *Teachers College Record* [online]. Available at www.tcrecord.org.

Archibald, Jo-Ann (1995). To Keep the Fire Going: The Challenge for First Nations Education in the Year 2000. In Ratna Ghosh and Douglas Ray (eds.), *Social Change and Education in Canada* (3rd edn). Toronto, ON: Harcourt Brace.

Aronowitz, Stanley (1992). *The Politics of Identity: Class, Culture, Social Movements.* New York, NY: Routledge.

Ashcroft, Bill, Griffiths, Gareth, and Tiffin, Helen, eds. (1995). *The Post-Colonial Studies Reader.* New York, NY: Routledge.

Assembly of First Nations (2002) [online]. Available at www.afn.ca/programs/education/educationsec.htm

Bang, Grace (2002). Watching Words and Managing Multiple Identities. In Linda Darling-Hammond, Jennifer French, and Silvia Garcia-Lopez, eds., *Learning to Teach for Social Justice.* New York, NY: Teachers College Press.

Banks, James (1993). The Canon Debate, Knowledge Construction, and Multicultural Education. *Educational Researcher* (June-July), 4–14.

Banks, James (1997). *Educating Citizens in a Multicultural Society.* New York, NY: Teachers College Press.

Battiste, Marie (1998). Enabling the Autumn Seed: Toward a Decolonized Approach to Aboriginal Knowledge, Language, and Education. *Canadian Journal of Native Education* 22(1), 16–27.

Battiste, Marie (2000). Introduction: Unfolding the Lessons of Colonization. In Marie Battiste (ed.), *Reclaiming Indigenous Voice and Vision.* Vancouver, BC: UBC Press.

Bauman, Zygmunt (2002). Global Solidarity, *Tikkun* 17:1.

Bennett, Christine (1999). *Comprehensive Multicultural Education: Theory and Practice* (4th edn). Boston, MA: Allyn and Bacon.

Bergman, Brian (1993). A Nation of Polite Bigots? *Maclean's* 106(52), 42–43.

Bernstein, Basil (1971). *Class, Codes and Control*. London, UK: Routledge.

Bhabha, Homi (1994). *The Location of Culture*. London, UK: Routledge.

Bourdieu, Pierre (1973). Cultural Reproduction and Social Reproduction. In Richard Brown (ed.), *Knowledge, Education and Cultural Change*. London, UK: Tavistock.

Bourdieu, Pierre and Passeron, Jean-Claude (1990). *Reproduction in Education, Society, and Culture*. London, UK: Sage.

Bowles, Samuel and Gintis, Herbert (1976). *Schooling in Capitalist America: Educational Reform and the Contradictions of Economic Life*. New York, NY: Basic Books.

Breton, Raymond (1991). *The Governance of Ethnic Communities: Political Structures and Processes in Canada*. New York, NY: Greenwood Press.

Bullivant, Brian (1981). *The Pluralist Dilemma in Education: Six Case Studies*. Sydney: George Allen and Unwin.

Capra, Fritjof (1991). *The Tao of Physics* (3rd edn). Boston, MA: Shambhala.

Carby, Hazel (1992). The Multicultural Wars. *Radical History Review* 54 (1992 Fall), 7–18.

Carlson, Dennis (1997). *Making Progress: Education and Culture in New Times*. New York, NY: Teachers College Press.

Carty, Linda (1991). Women's Studies in Canada: A Discourse and Praxis of Exclusion. *Resources for Feminist Research* 20(3/4), 12–18.

Chomsky, Noam (2001). 9-11. New York, NY: Seven Stories Press.

Clairmont, Donald and Magill, Dennis (1999). *Africville: The Life and Death of a Canadian Black Community*. Toronto: Canadian Scholars' Press.

Collins, Patricia (2000). *Black Feminist Thought: Knowledge, Consciousness and the Politics of Empowerment* (2nd revision, 10th Anniversary edn). New York, NY: Routledge.

Cornbleth, Catherine and Waugh, Dexter (1995). *The Great Speckled Bird: Multicultural Politics and Education Policymaking*. New York, NY: St. Martin's Press.

Council of Canadians (1998). *Confronting Globalization and Reclaiming Democracy*. Ottawa.

Courts, Patrick (1997). *Multicultural Literacies: Dialect, Discourse and Diversity*. New York, NY: Peter Lang.

Darling-Hammond, Linda (2002). Learning to Teach for Social Justice. In Linda Darling-Hammond, Jennifer French, and Silvia Garcia-Lopez (eds.), *Learning to Teach for Social Justice*. New York, NY: Teachers College Press.

Davidman, Leonard and Davidman, Patricia (2000). *Teaching with a Multicultural Perspective: A Practical Guide* (3rd edn). Toronto, ON: Longman.

Dei, George (1996). *Anti-Racism Education: Theory and Practice*. Halifax, NS: Fernwood Publishing.

De Lauretis, Teresa (1987). *Technologies of Gender*. Bloomington, IN: Indiana University Press.

Derrida, Jacques (1976). *Of Grammatology* (G. Spivak, Trans.). Baltimore, MD: John Hopkins University Press.

Derrida, Jacques (1973). *Speech and Phenomena, and other Essays on Husserl's Theory of Signs* (D.B. Allison, Trans.). Evanston, IL: Northwestern University Press.

Dewey, John (1929). *Democracy and Education: An Introduction to the Philosophy of Education*. New York, NY: Macmillan.

Dewey, John (1952). *Experience and Education*. New York, NY: Macmillan.

Diamond, Barbara and Moore, Margaret (1995). *Multicultural Literacy: Mirroring the Reality of the Classroom*. New York, NY: Longman.

Edelsky, Carole (1990). Whose Agenda is this Anyway? A Response to McKenna, Robinson, and Miller. *Educational Researcher* 19(8), 7–11.

Elliott, Jean Leonard and Fleras, Augie (1990). Immigration and the Canadian Ethnic Mosaic. In P. S. Li (ed.), *Race and Ethnic Relations in Canada*. Toronto, ON: Oxford University Press.

Elshtain, Jean Bethke (1993). *Democracy on Trial*. Concord, ON: Anansi Press.

Enslin, Penny (1999). Education for Liberal Democracy: Universalising a Western Construct? *Journal of Philosophy of Education* 33(2), 175–186.

Erikson, Erik (1963). *Childhood and Society* (2nd edn). New York, NY: Norton.

Fanon, Frantz (1967). *Black Skin, White Masks*. New York, NY: Grove Press.

Fanon, Frantz (1968). *The Wretched of the Earth*. New York, NY: Grove Press.

Freire, Paulo (2000). *Pedagogy of the Oppressed* (M. Bergman Ramos, Trans.) (30th Anniversary edn). New York, NY: Continuum.

Freire, Paulo (1985). *The Politics of Education: Culture, Power, and Liberation* (D. Macedo, Trans.). South Hadley, MA: Bergin and Garvey.

Freire, Paulo (1998). *Politics and Education* (P. Lindquist Wong, Trans.). Los Angeles, CA: UCLA Latin American Center Publications.

Fukuyama, Francis (1992). *The End of History and the Last Man*. New York, NY: Free Press.

Gaskell, Jane, McLaren, Arlene, and Novogrodsky, Myra (1989). *Claiming an Education: Feminism and Canadian Schools*. Toronto, ON: Our Schools, Our Selves.

Ghosh, Ratna (1996). *Redefining Multicultural Education*. Toronto, ON: Harcourt Brace.

Ghosh, Ratna and Tarrow, Norma (1993). Multiculturalism and Teacher Education: Views from Canada and the USA. *Comparative Education* 29(1), 81–92.

Ghosh, Ratna, Fox, Christine, Tarrow, Norma, and Luchtenberg, Sigrid (1995). From Theory to Policy and Practice in Multicultural Education. Unpublished paper presented at the Annual Conference of the Comparative Education Society (US). March, Boston, MA.

Gibbins, Roger and Youngman, Loleen (1996). *Mindscapes: Political Ideologies Towards the 21st Century*. Toronto, ON: McGraw-Hill.

Gilligan, Carol (1982). *In a Different Voice*. Cambridge, MA: Harvard University Press.

Gilroy, Paul (1990). One Nation Under a Groove: The Cultural Politics of "Race" and Racism in Britain. In D. Goldberg (ed.), *Anatomy of Racism*. Minneapolis, MN: University of Minnesota Press.

Giroux, Henry (1981). *Ideology, Culture and the Process of Schooling*. Philadelphia, PA: Temple University Press.

Giroux, Henry (1991). Postmodernism As Border Pedagogy: Redefining the Boundaries of Race and Ethnicity. In Henry Giroux (ed.), *Postmodernism, Feminism and Cultural Politics: Redrawing Educational Boundaries*. Albany, NY: State University of New York Press.

Giroux, Henry (1992). *Border Crossings: Cultural Workers and the Politics of Education*. New York, NY: Routledge.

Giroux, Henry (1993). Living Dangerously: Identity Politics and the New Cultural Racism: Towards a Critical Pedagogy of Representation. *Cultural Studies* 7(1), 1–27.

Giroux, Henry (1997). *Pedagogy and the Politics of Hope: Theory, Culture and Schooling: A Critical Reader*. Boulder, CO: Westview.

Giroux, Henry (2000). *Impure Acts: The Practical Politics of Cultural Studies*. New York, NY: Routledge.

Giroux, Henry (2001). *Public Spaces, Private Lives: Beyond the Culture of Cynicism*. Lanham, MD: Rowman and Littlefield.

Giroux, Henry (2002). Democracy, Freedom and Justice after September 11th: Rethinking the Role of Educators and the Politics of Schooling. *Teachers College Record* [online]. Available at www.tcrecord.org.

Goldberg, David (1992). The Semantics of Race. *Ethnic and Racial Studies* 15(4), 543–569.

Goldberg, David (1994). Introduction: Multicultural Conditions. In David Goldberg (ed.), *Multiculturalism: A Critical Reader*. Cambridge, MA: Blackwell.

Goldberg, David (2002). *The Racial State*. Malden, MA: Blackwell

Gore, Jennifer (1993). *The Struggle for Pedagogies: Critical and Feminist Discourses As Regimes of Truth*. New York, NY: Routledge.

Government of Canada (1867). The Constitution Act, 1867 (The British North America Act, 1867).

Government of Canada (1982). Canadian Charter of Rights and Freedoms. Schedule B Constitution Act, 1982 (79)

Government of Canada (1988). Canadian Multiculturalism Act. Statutes of Canada. c.31

Gramsci, Antonio (1990). *Selections from the Prison Notebooks.* (Quintin Hoare and Geoffrey Smith, trans. and eds.). Minneapolis, MN: University of Minnesota Press.

Gramsci, Antonio (1988). *Gramsci's Prison Letters: A Selection* (H. Henderson, trans.). London, UK: Zwan in association with the *Edinburgh Review.*

Greene, M. (1993). The Passions of Pluralism: Multiculturalism and the Expanding Community. *Educational Researcher* 22(1), 13–18.

Habermas, Jürgen (1992). Citizenship and National Identity: Some Reflections on the Future of Europe. *Praxis International* 12(1), 1–19.

Habermas, Jürgen (1979). *Communication and the Evolution of Society* (Thomas McCarthy, trans.). Boston, MA: Beacon Press.

Hall, Stuart (1990). Cultural Identity and Diaspora. In J. Rutherford (ed.), *Identity: Community, Culture, Difference.* London, UK: Lawrence and Wishart.

Hall, Stuart (1997). The Local and the Global: Globalization and Ethnicity. In Anne McClintock, Amir Mufti, and Ella Shohat (eds.), *Dangerous Liaisons: Gender, Nation and Postcolonial Perspectives.* Minneapolis, MN: University of Minnesota Press.

Hartman, Geoffrey (1997). *The Fateful Question of Culture.* New York, NY: Columbia University Press.

Hartstock, Nancy (1987). Rethinking Modernism: Minority vs. Majority Theories. *Cultural Critique* 7, 187–206.

hooks, bell (1984). *Feminist Theory from Margin to Center.* Boston, MA: South End Press

Horkheimer, Max (1972). *Critical Theory* (Matthew O'Connell, trans). New York, NY: Herder and Herder.

Huntington, Samuel (1993). The Clash of Civilizations? *Foreign Affairs* 72(3), 22–49.

Huntington, Samuel (1996). *The Clash of Civilizations and the Remaking of World Order*. New York, NY: Simon and Schuster.

Julien, Isaac and Mercer, Kobena (1988). De Margin and De Centre. *Screen* 29(4), 2–10.

Kagawa, Joy (1993). What Do I Remember of the Evacuation. In Eva Karpinski and Ian Lea (eds.), *Pens of Many Colours*. Toronto, ON: Harcourt Brace Jovanovich.

Kirkness, Verna (1998). The Critical State of Aboriginal Languages in Canada. *Canadian Journal of Native Education* 22(1), 93–107.

Kovel, Joel (1984). *White Racism: A Psychohistory* (2nd edn). New York, NY: Columbia University Press.

Krishnan, Analya and Berry, J.W. (1992). Acculturative Stress and Acculturation Attitudes among Indian Immigrants to the United States. *Psychology and Developing Societies* 4(2), 187–212.

Kuhn, Thomas (1996). *The Structure of Scientific Revolutions* (3rd edn). Chicago, IL: University of Chicago Press.

Jiyu, Ren, ed. (1993). A Taoist Classic: The Book of Lao Zi. Beijing: Foreign Languages Press.

Lautard, Hugh and Guppy, Neil (1990). Revisiting the Vertical Mosaic: Occupational Stratification among Canadian Ethnic Groups. In Peter S. Li (ed.), *Race and Ethnic Relations in Canada*. Toronto, ON: Oxford University Press.

Leistyna, Pepi (1997). Racenicity: Whitewashing Ethnicity. *The Review of Education/Pedagogy/Cultural Studies* 19(2/3), 269–295.

Lessard, Claude and Crespo, Manuel (1992). Multicultural Education in Canada: Policies and Practices. In Douglas Ray and Deo Poonwassie (eds.), *Education and Cultural Differences: New Perspectives*. New York, NY: Garland Publishing.

Lewis, Magda (1990). Interrupting Patriarchy: Politics, Resistance, and Transformation in the Feminist Classroom. *Harvard Educational Review* 60(4), 467–88.

Lorde, Audre (1984). *Sister Outsider*. Trumansburg, NY: Crossing Press.

Luke, Carmen and Gore, Jennifer, eds. (1992). *Feminisms and Critical*

Pedagogy. New York, NY: Routledge.

Lusted, David (1986). Why pedagogy? *Screen* 27(5), 2–14.

Lyotard, Jean-Francois (1984). *The Postmodern Condition: A Report on Knowledge* (G. Bennington and B. Massumi, trans.). Minneapolis, MN: University of Minnesota Press.

Mackey, Eva (1998). *The House of Difference: Cultural Politics and National Identity in Canada*. New York, NY: Routledge.

Macedo, Donaldo (1995). Literacy for Stupidification: The Pedagogy of the Big Lies. In Christine Sleeter and Peter McLaren (eds.), *Multicultural Education, Critical Pedagogy, and the Politics of Difference*. Albany, NY: State University of New York Press.

Marcuse, Herbert (1964). *One-Dimensional Man*. Boston, MA: Beacon Press.

Matustik, Martin (1998). *Specters of Liberation: Great Refusals in the New World Order*. Albany, NY: State University of New York Press.

Mayo, Peter (1999). *Gramsci, Freire and Adult Education: Possibilities for Transformative Action*. London, UK: Zed Books.

McAndrew, Marie (1985). Le traitement du racisme, de l'immigration et de la réalité multi-ethnique dans les manuels scolaires francophones au Québec. Monograph, Minority Education Project. Montreal, QC: McGill University.

McAndrew, Marie (1993). The Integration of Ethnic Minority Students Fifteen Years after Bill 101: Some Issues Confronting the Montreal Island French Language Public Schools. R.F. Harnie Program on Immigration and Ethnicity Working Papers. Toronto, ON: University of Toronto.

McLaren, Peter (1994). *Critical Pedagogy and Predatory Culture: Oppositional Politics in a Postmodern Era*. New York, NY: Routledge.

McLaren, Peter (1997). *Revolutionary Multiculturalism: Pedagogies of Dissent for the New Millennium*. Boulder, CO: Westview Press.

McLaren, Peter (1998). Revolutionary Pedagogy in Post-Revolutionary Times: Rethinking the Political Economy of Critical Education. *Educational Theory* 48(4), 431–462.

McRobbie, Angela (1991). *Feminism and Youth Culture*. Houndmills, UK: Macmillan.

Memmi, Albert (1991 [1957]). *The Colonizer and the Colonized*. Boston, MA: Beacon Press.

Mercer, Cecil (1992). *Students with Learning Disabilities*. New York, NY: Maxwell Macmillan International.

Minow, Martha (1990). *Making all the Difference: Inclusion, Exclusion, and American Law*. Ithaca, NY: Cornell University Press.

Mohanty, Chandra (1990). On Race and Voice: Challenges for Liberal Education in the 1990s. *Cultural Critique* 14 (Winter 1989/90), 179–208.

Mohanty, Chandra (1995). Under Western Eyes: Feminist Scholarship and Colonial Discourses. In Bill Ashcroft, Helen Tiffin, and Gareth Griffiths (eds.), *The Post-Colonial Studies Reader*. New York, NY: Routledge.

Morrison, Toni (1993). *Playing in the Dark: Whiteness and the Literary Imagination*. New York, NY: Vintage

Muszynski, Alicja (1991). What is Patriarchy? In Jesse Vorst et al. (eds.), *Race, Class, Gender: Bonds and Barriers*. Toronto, ON: Garamond Press.

Nandy, A. (1997). Colonization of the Mind. In M. Rahnema and V. Bowtree (eds.), *The Post-Development Reader*. London, UK: Zed Books.

Narayan, Uma and Harding, Sandra (2000). *Decentering the Center: Philosophy for a Multicultural, Postcolonial, and Feminist World*. Bloomington, IN: Indiana University Press.

Ng, Roxana (1993). A Woman out of Control: Deconstructing Sexism and Racism in the University. *Canadian Journal of Education* 18(3), 189–205.

Nieto, Sonia (1992). *Affirming Diversity: The Sociopolitical Context of Multicultural Education*. New York, NY: Longman.

Nussbaum, Martha (1998*). Cultivating Humanity: Classical Defense of Reform in Liberal Education*. Cambridge, MA: Harvard University Press.

Ogbu, John (1992). Understanding Cultural Diversity and Learning. *Educational Researcher* 21(8), 5–14.

Palmer, John and Hines, Melanie (2003). *Review: Ethnicity, Race and Nationality in Education: A Global Perspective* (2001) by Ken

Shimahara et al. Mahwah, NJ: L. Erlbaum Associates. *Teachers College Record* [online]. Available at www.tcrecord.org.

Phinney, Jean (1990). Ethnic Identity in Adolescents and Adults: Review of Research. *Psychological Bulletin* 108(3), 499–514.

Pearson, A.T. (1989). *The Teacher: Theory and Practice in Teacher Education*. New York, NY: Routledge.

Quebec (1981). *Autant de façons d'être Québécois; plan d'action du gouvernement du Québec a l'intention de communautés culturelles*. Quebec, QC: Ministère des Communautés Culturelles et de l'Immigration.

Quebec (1990). *Let's Build Quebec Together: A Policy Statement on Immigration and Integration*. Montreal, QC: Ministère des Communautés Culturelles et de l'Immigration du Québec.

Quebec (1998a). *A School for the Future: Policy Statement on Educational Integration and Intercultural Education*. Quebec, QC: Ministère de l'Éducation.

Quebec (1998b). *Plan of Action for Educational Integration and Intercultural Education 1998–2002*. Quebec, QC: Ministère de l'Éducation.

Rawls, John (1971). *A Theory of Justice*. Cambridge, MA: Belknap Press.

Renan, Ernest (1990). What Is a Nation? In Homi Bhabha (ed.), *Nation and Narration*. New York, NY: Routledge.

Rich, Adrienne (1986). Notes Toward a Politics of Location. In Adrienne Rich (ed.), *Blood, Bread and Poetry: Selected Prose 1979–1985*. New York, NY: W.W. Norton and Co.

Rorty. Richard (1991). *Objectivism, Relativism, and Truth*. Cambridge, UK: Cambridge University Press.

Ruiz, A. (2002). Wanted: Teachers with *Conciencia*. In Linda Darling-Hammond, Jennifer French, and Silvia Garcia-Lopez (eds.), *Learning to Teach for Social Justice*. New York, NY: Teachers College Press.

Rutherford, Jonathan (1990). *Identity: Community, Culture, Difference*. London, UK: Lawrence and Wishart.

Said, Edward (1989). Representing the Colonized: Anthropology's Interlocutors. *Critical Inquiry* 15(2), 205–225.

Said, Edward (1993). *Culture and Imperialism*. New York, NY: Knopf.

Said, Edward (2000). *Reflections on Exile and Other Essays*. Cambridge, MA: Harvard University Press.

Sárkány, Mihaly (1992). Modernization, Cultural Pluralism and Identity: An Approach from Cultural Anthropology. *Prospects* 22(1), 21–30.

Saul, John Ralston (2001). *On Equilibrium*. Toronto, ON: Viking.

Scheurich, James Joseph (1993). Toward a White Discourse on White Racism. *Educational Researcher* (November), 5–10.

Scott, Fentey (2001). *Teaching in a Multicultural Setting: A Canadian Perspective*. Toronto, ON: Prentice-Hall.

Sen, Amartya. (2002). East and West in the Media. Address to the World Newspaper Congress, Belgium May 26 and 29.

Singh, Raja Roy (1992). Changing Education for a Changing World. *Prospects* 22(1), 7–18.

Sleeter, Christine (1991). *Empowerment through Multicultural Education*. Albany, NY: State University of New York Press.

Smith, William, Foster, William, and Donahue, Helen (1999). *The Contemporary Education Scene in Québec: A Handbook for Policy Makers, Administrators and Educators*. Montreal, QC: Office of Research on Educational Policy, McGill University.

Snauwaert, Dale (2002). Cosmopolitan Democracy and Democratic Education. *Current Issues in Comparative Education* [online]. Available at www.tc.columbia.edu/cice/

Somers, Patricia and Somers-Willett, Susan (2002). Collateral Damage: Faculty Free Speech in America After 9/11. *Teachers College Record* [online]. Available at www.tcrecord.org.

Stam, Robert and Shohat, Ella (1995). Contested Histories: Eurocentrism, Multiculturalism, and the Media. In David Goldberg (ed.), *Multiculturalism: A Critical Reader*. Cambridge, MA: Blackwell.

Stromquist, Nelly (2002). Globalization, the I, and the Other. *Current Issues in Comparative Education* 4(2) [online]. Available at www.tc.columbia.edu/cice/.

Taylor, Charles (1994). The Politics of Recognition. In D. Goldberg (ed.), *Multiculturalism: A Critical Reader*. Cambridge, MA: Blackwell.

Tilak, Jandhyala (1994). *Education for Development in Asia*. New Delhi: Sage.

Torczyner, James L. et al. (1997). *Diversity, Mobility and Change: The Dynamics of Black Communities in Canada*. Montreal, QC: McGill Consortium for Ethnicity and Strategic Planning, Executive Summary Presented to the Multiculturalism Branch, Department of Canadian Heritage, Ottawa, 1997.

Trudeau, Pierre Elliott (1971). Bilingualism Within a Multicultural Framework. Available at http://www.canadahistory.com/sections/documents/.

Office of the High Commissioner for Human Rights (1965). International Convention on the Elimination of All Forms of Racial Discrimination. (Entry into force January 1969.)

Walker, James (1992). South Asians in Canadian Immigration Policy: An Historical Overview. In Ratna Ghosh and Rabindra Kanungo (eds.), *South Asian Canadians: Current Issues in the Politics of Culture*. Calgary, AB: Shastri Indo-Canadian Institute.

Weiler, Kathleen (1991). Freire and a Feminist Pedagogy of Difference. *Harvard Educational Review* 61(4), 449–474.

Welch, Sharon (1991). An Ethic of Solidarity and Difference. In H.A. Giroux (ed.), *Postmodernism, Feminism, and Cultural Politics*. Albany, NY: State University of New York Press.

West, Cornel (1993). The New Cultural Politics of Difference. In S. During (ed.), *The Cultural Studies Reader*. New York, NY: Routledge.

Williamson, John (1993). Democracy and the "Washington Consensus." *World Development* 21(8), 1329–1336.

Willis, Paul (1977). *Learning to Labour: How Working Class Kids Get Working Class Jobs*. Farnborough, UK: Saxon House.

Young, Iris (1990). *Justice and the Politics of Difference*. Princeton, NJ: Princeton University Press.

Dr. Ratna Ghosh is James McGill Professor and William C. Macdonald Professor of Education at McGill University in Montreal, where she was formerly Dean of Education. She was appointed Member of the Order of Canada in 2000, and was elected a Fellow of the Royal Society of Canada in 1999. She is also a Member of the European Academy of Arts, Sciences, and Humanities. Her previous books include *Redefining Multicultural Education* and *Social Change and Education in Canada.*

Dr. Ali A. Abdi received his PhD from McGill University in 1998, and is Associate Professor of Education at the University of Alberta in Edmonton. He is also the author of *Culture, Education and Development in South Africa: Historical and Contemporary Perspectives.*